THE BRONX

in the Innocent Years
1890–1925

THE
IN THE INNOCENT

LLOYD ULTAN &

Written in collaboration with

BRONX

YEARS, 1890-1925

GARY HERMALYN

The Bronx County Historical Society

HARPER & ROW, PUBLISHERS, New York
Cambridge, Philadelphia, San Francisco, London
Mexico City, São Paulo, Singapore, Sydney

1817

To the memoir writers,
who left as their legacy
their time in words

The chapters in this book originally appeared as articles in *The Bronx County Historical Society Journal.* Except where noted, all photographs are reproduced by the courtesy of The Bronx County Historical Society Collection.

FIRST EDITION

Designer: Abigail Sturges

Library of Congress Cataloging in Publication Data

Ultan, Lloyd.
   The Bronx in the innocent years (1890–1925)

   Includes index.
    1. Bronx (New York, N.Y.)—Social life and customs.
2. Bronx (New York, N.Y.)—Biography. 3. Bronx (New York, N.Y.)—Description. 4. New York (N.Y.)—Social life and customs. 5. New York (N.Y.)—Biography. 6. New York (N.Y.)—Description. I. Hermalyn, Gary. II. Bronx County Historical Society. III. Title.
F128.68.B8U583   1985   974.7'275041   84-48200
ISBN 0-06-015419-5

85 86 87 88 89 MPC 10 9 8 7 6 5 4 3 2 1

Contents

Foreword

EDWARD I. KOCH
Mayor of The City of New York

As mayor of New York, the greatest city in the world, and as an author myself, I always keep an eye out for books about this wonderful metropolis. Many books focus only on Manhattan. A few years ago, however, I was delighted to receive a copy of *The Beautiful Bronx (1920–1950),* written by Lloyd Ultan in collaboration with The Bronx County Historical Society. Here at last was a book that gave well-deserved attention to one of the city's other four boroughs.

Now that same combination, joined by Gary Hermalyn, has produced another fascinating book, *The Bronx in the Innocent Years, 1890–1925.* People who lived in The Bronx in that era present their own firsthand accounts of the things they did and saw. They came from many different ethnic groups and were constantly confronted by change and innovation. Trolley cars, elevated trains and the invention of automobiles drastically altered the course of their lives. Their reminiscences preserve forever the experience of growing up in The Bronx when that borough was changing from a rural area to a suburb, and from a suburb to a city.

I can appreciate their experiences because I was born in The Bronx in the innocent years. The apartment house in which I lived on Crotona Park East faced one of the great parks of The Bronx and of New York City: Crotona Park. For my parents and their neighbors, it was both a front yard and a playground. Indeed, the neighborhood had the feeling of a village filled with hardworking people who looked to the future with hope and optimism. Their story, and the stories of the people whose recollections have been recorded for this book, are typical of the people who lived in The Bronx, and in the other boroughs of New York City. Their lives tell the story of America.

Acknowledgments

This work was produced because of the selfless efforts of the early volunteers of The Bronx County Historical Society. For their dedication, understanding, direction, and assistance we sincerely thank Bert Gumpert, Theodore Kazimiroff, Theodore Schliessman, Bert Sack, Robert Farkas, Joseph J. Nardone, Doris Schneible, George Tabor, George Fluhr, May A. Doherty, John McNamara, Erich Marks, Roger Arcara, Thomas Mullins, George Zoebelein, Ron Schleissman, Dominick R. Massaro, Edward Wolf, Jean Milsner, Edna Fassig, Sanford Lent, Sol Elbaum, and all the other unsung people who gave their all to the history of The Bronx.

We also acknowledge with gratitude the services or donations of Arthur Seifert, Laura Tosi, Kay Gleeson, Mary Ilario, Rose Politi, Ray Beckerman, Nicholas DiBrino, Roger Wines, Peter Derrick, Grace Higgs Reel, Edna Mead, Jay Filan, David Meth, Raymond and Mary Crapo, J. Podgor, Bill Kanski, L. Mangiarotti, Elizabeth Beirne, Robert Hall, Natalie Esnard, Walter Fitzgerald, Brother Edward Quinn, Lisa Seifert, Terry Seifert, the Astoria Motion Picture Foundation, Wave Hill, Aquinas High School, the Huntington Free Library and Reading Room, the Library of Congress, the New York *Daily News,* Manhattan College Archives, New York University, New York Zoological Society, and Fordham University Archives.

Introduction

The decades from 1890 to 1925 were the innocent years in The Bronx. During that period The Bronx grew from an area of small villages and farms to a borough of the nation's greatest metropolis, housing more than one million people. This rapid growth and the changes it brought in its train were almost universally looked upon by the area's residents as signs of progress. The Bronx was on the move, and the future was promising.

Despite the rise of settlement in The Bronx and the alterations in landscape and lifestyle that characterized the era, traditional values and relationships between people and their families, their friends, their institutions, and their localities survived almost intact from the simpler rural era that preceded it. An innocent faith in the absolute positive value of change was, in fact, part of that heritage. People living in The Bronx between 1890 and 1925 perceived the world as constantly improving, without realizing that change itself would eventually radically alter their way of life.

In 1890, the section of the New York mainland north and east of the Harlem River was under two jurisdictions. The area west of the Bronx River had been annexed to New York City in 1874 to form the Twenty-third and Twenty-fourth wards of the metropolis. The land east of the river remained a part of Westchester County until 1895, when it, too, was annexed to the growing city and included in the Twenty-fourth Ward. The newly combined region was referred to as the Annexed District or the North Side until 1898, when it was officially designated as the borough of The Bronx, after the river that coursed through its center.

To the people living in The Bronx at that time, becoming part of the most dynamic city on the face of the earth was an occasion for pride. Despite their new citizenship, however, Bronxites continued to lead everyday lives that were almost provincial. When asked where he lived, a Bronx resident would invariably reply Mott Haven, or Westchester, or Kingsbridge, or Morrisania, or whatever small village happened to be his home.

During the last decade of the nineteenth century, there was little difference between one Bronx village and the next, except, perhaps, for their size. The typical village encompassed only a few blocks and was separated from its neighbors by empty lots and fields of plowed farmland, orchards, or meadows. Its streets were usually narrow dirt roads, and while more important thoroughfares were wider and likely to be macadamized, this was not necessarily true of all of them. For example, Central Avenue (later renamed Jerome Avenue) was a dirt road, except for one stretch that was made of sand.

Each village had one street where at least one general store could be found, as was true of Springhurst on Hunt's Point. Larger villages were blessed with a street offering a variety of shops and services. Riverdale Avenue in Kingsbridge had a grocery, a vegetable store, an ice cream parlor, and two bakeries, as well as a blacksmith, two plumbers, a major coalyard, and a canner, until most of these businesses were swept away in a disastrous fire in 1903. In the first decade of the century, Willis Avenue became a local shopping street in Mott Haven, with shops located in stores provided at the street level of a series of four-story walk-up apartment buildings. Here could be found beer gardens, saloons, bicycle repair shops, groceries, and a wide variety of other services. Tremont Avenue between Park and Third avenues featured a Western Union telegraph office, a jeweler, a cigar store, and restaurants, along with stores similar to those found on Willis Avenue.

No one in the borough characterized himself as being poor; like most Americans at this time, Bronxites considered themselves to be part of the great middle class. With rare exceptions, most Bronx residents owned their own homes, rather than renting them, and they lived in frame houses. The few individuals who were wealthy showed their affluence in their style of living. Riverdale, one area where the well-to-do congregated, was home to families such as the Dodges, the Delafields, and the Pynes, who owned great mansions situated on large landscaped estates. Another affluent section was Throggs Neck. Here Collis P. Huntington, the owner of several railroads around the country, and John A. Morris, who raised thoroughbred racehorses, dwelt during the summer in their waterfront mansions.

While there was not much ethnic diversity in any given Bronx village, some did have a greater concentration of one ethnic group than another. For example, in Morrisania the population was predominantly German, immigration from Germany to America having begun about forty years earlier. Morrisania's Germans would attend either the Lutheran or the Catholic church every Sunday with their American-born children. Another area heavily settled by the Germans was Melrose, whose main street, Courtlandt Avenue, was called "Dutch Broadway" because of the concentration of German shops, saloons, beer halls, and gymnastic and singing societies. ("Dutch," a corruption of the word *deutsch,* was a popular term for Germans.)

In Mott Haven, the majority was made up by the Irish, who worked in the Mott Iron Foundry or the Stephens Coal Yard. Irish doctors settled on Alexander Avenue, and their wealth gave this street of decorative attached town houses the nickname "Irish Fifth Avenue." The Irish were also a strong presence in Kingsbridge, and in Riverdale served on estates as gardeners and servants or worked in the shops along Riverdale Avenue. Here, however, their numbers were equaled by long-established Anglo-Saxon families.

A few German and Irish families could in fact be found in almost every village at the time, and while other ethnic groups were represented, none was as dominant. In the first decade of the new century, a number of black families lived near 163rd Street in Morrisania, and a small population of blacks began to concentrate in an area of substantial homes in Williamsbridge. In Mott Haven, the Baron de Hirsch Fund purchased land in the vicinity of Brown Place, where it settled some Jews. Families of Jews could also be found in Hunt's Point and Morrisania.

A Bronx village was a very tight-knit community, and everyone knew his neighbors. Most people not only lived in their village but worked there as well. The family doctor, who made house calls in his horse and buggy (switching to a horseless carriage as the new century progressed), was usually near at hand. The schoolteacher was a neighbor. Owners of the grocery stores, blacksmith shops, saloons, coalyards, and breweries usually lived close to their establishments. Workingmen who toiled in the Johnson Iron Foundry, the Ebling Brewery, the American Bank Note Company, the Bolton Bleachery, or the area's many piano factories were villagers who walked to work each morning.

Women toiled as well. At the turn of the century, daily cooking and keeping house were quite a chore. Every Monday, washing was done by scraping soap into a large copper-bottomed kettle filled with boiling water. After the clothes were placed in the kettle, the water was swirled with a broomstick. Rinsed, then wrung out, the wash was placed in a wicker basket, taken out into the backyard, and hung on the clothesline to dry. Tuesdays were devoted to ironing. It was only on Wednesday that women would set aside their work for socializing, visiting one another's homes, exchanging news of the family.

Children, through no lack of love from their families, were generally left to themselves. After coming home from school and changing into clothes fit for the hurly-burly of street games, they might eat a slice of bread with homemade jelly on it, and then dash outdoors and play with their friends in the village.

Generally, sports were not highly organized. Boys would play a pickup game of baseball, or a version of the sport called cat, which involved each boy in his turn using a broomstick to hit a small stick with a pointed end as far as possible. Fighting was usually discouraged, but it was taken for granted that boys would brawl with one another. Whenever such a display of streetside fisticuffs ended, each participant seemed to achieve respect in the other's eyes, and the fight often closed with a friendly handshake. Those who lived near the waterside could go fishing and, in the flat sands of the shore of Long Island Sound, clamming.

Girls were raised with a view to becoming good housewives and mothers. In addition to aiding in the household chores, every girl was expected to learn some of the refined graces, especially playing the piano and singing. Despite the practical bent of their upbringing, girls were allowed plenty of time to have fun. Wealthier families might give their daughters dolls with bisque heads, while those who could not afford that extravagance would choose rag dolls.

The center of life for all children was the school. At the turn of the century, the rigors of merely getting to school helped inculcate discipline in a child. Boys and girls from Hunt's Point, for example, had to walk miles through fields and empty lots to reach their classes in Mott Haven, since no school nearer to them existed. In the town of Westchester and its outlying areas, pupils had to board a stagecoach to travel to the small four-room schoolhouse on Throggs Neck.

Whether run by public authorities or under religious auspices, the schools not only drilled the traditional "three Rs" daily, but stressed penmanship and deportment as well. In those days, elementary school lasted until the eighth grade, and provided every pupil an education sufficient to deal with the world in which he or she was expected to work upon graduation. Very few students were expected to go on to high school, which was considered higher education and was called "the people's college."

Those graduates of elementary schools who did wish further education could not go on to high school within The Bronx until the Mixed High School, later named Morris High School, opened in 1897. Public leaders, incensed that the city's Board of Education had intended to name the first such institution in the new borough after Peter Cooper, insisted that a more appropriate choice would be Gouverneur Morris, who was not only identified with The Bronx but was famous as a framer of the Constitution of the United States. When the growing population made it necessary that another high school be opened, strong public sentiment urged that it be named for Evander Childs, a beloved Bronx educator who had died at his principal's desk in a Bronx public school.

Although secondary education was a relatively late arrival in The Bronx, higher education had already been well established by 1890. St. John's College, run by the Jesuits, had been a fixture of the village that grew up around the Fordham station of the New York Central Railroad since 1841. It seemed only fitting that when it received university status, in the first decade of the twentieth century, it should change its name to Fordham. In the north of Riverdale, girls could attend the Academy of Mount Saint Vincent, which was run by the Sisters of Charity and which attained college status early in the new century. The first secular institution of higher education in The Bronx was established shortly before the old century closed when New York University built a new campus (with buildings designed by the noted architect Stanford White) in an area overlooking the Harlem River valley. The chancellor who had made the decision to locate the campus there, Henry Mitchell MacCracken, took a leading part in the cultural and civic life of the fledgling borough. He also coined the name University Heights for the land around the campus, which had previously held only the estates of wealthy merchants. MacCracken himself moved into one of the mansions just north of the new university. In 1923, the Christian Brothers instituted a new campus of Manhattan College atop a hill overlooking Van Cortlandt Park, giving The Bronx its fourth college.

While work and school occupied a large part of the average Bronxite's life during these years, time was set aside for fun. Most people found diversion in everyday pursuits near home. Books were read avidly, often aloud to the entire family in the evening. The availability of books grew with the establishment of local public libraries, often aided by money provided by Andrew Carnegie. One such library opened at Alexander Avenue and 138th Street in Mott Haven, another on 169th Street near McKinley Square in Morrisania. Collis P. Huntington endowed a free library for the town of Westchester at Westchester Square in 1890.

Newspapers were also popular reading material, and two papers existed to report important occurrences to residents of The Bronx. The first, the *North Side News,* appealed mostly to businessmen and enjoyed its best years in the decade of the 1890s. Its leadership was challenged in 1907 by the lively *Bronx Home News,* which gave prominent coverage to local events. The paper grew quickly from a weekly publication to a semiweekly and then to a daily. In both newspapers, the political changes of the day were well chronicled. After the creation of the borough in 1898, they reported the agitation that led to the establishment of The Bronx as a separate county of the state. (The other city boroughs all had county status.) A new "borough" courthouse was built on 161st Street and Third Avenue in anticipation of housing the new county courts. It was in that building that the ceremonies inaugurating the new Bronx County were held in 1914.

Evenings that a family spent outside its home were special occasions. The beer gardens that abounded in The Bronx were favorite places for dinner and entertainment, and no one thought it unusual for parents to take their children to them, even though alcoholic beverages were served. While most of these establishments were located in the German enclaves of Morrisania and Melrose, the largest beer garden was owned by Adam Hoffmann in Throggs Neck. There, visitors could play baseball, bowl, and hold races, as well as eat and drink.

In the villages, entertainment could be found both in the home and within walking distance from it. In Bronx parlors at the turn of the century, women usually played the piano for family and guests, and family sing-alongs were also popular. The Germans formed singing societies which regularly practiced choral works and appeared at public functions. Not to be outdone, German musicians formed street bands, which frequently stopped at a saloon or a beer garden for refreshment as they traveled around the village.

Churches and schools put on amateur theatricals. Often these took the form of recitals of poetry by children, with appropriate gestures to emphasize a line. Professional performances were available only in the southernmost portion of the borough, particularly in Mott Haven. The first theatrical center was the Metropolis Theater on 142nd Street and Third Avenue. The resident company was led by Cecil Spooner, whose troupe put on many a show with an Irish theme that greatly pleased the village's Irish population. Germans appreciated the German operas performed at the Bronx Opera House.

By the early years of the twentieth century, new forms of entertainment were beginning to come into the villages as well. Motion pictures made their debut in small storefronts and in inexpensive nickelodeons. In the heat of a summer's night, silent films were played on a screen placed in an outdoor enclosure behind the theater to take advantage of cool breezes. Pillows were rented to the customers to help offset the hardness of the benches. Movies were even made in The Bronx. The Edison Studio opened on Oliver Place in Bedford Park, and in 1912, D. W. Griffith and the Biograph Studio began operation on 175th Street in Tremont. Local residents eagerly volunteered to appear in the crowd scenes.

This cozy and comfortable village life, with its rounds of familiar chores and scenes, with its nearby shops and factories, with its prevalence of homeowners living in single-family houses, often with chickens, pigs, and cows in the backyard and plots of land planted with vegetables for family consumption, was bound to change. And the greatest single engine of that change was the spread of the public transportation system.

In the 1890s, a resident of The Bronx had only a limited number of ways to travel. For local trips around the village and within a few miles of it, most people either walked or took a horse and carriage. Some villages, however, most notably those close to the southern end of the borough, were favored with horsecar service which would take riders to 129th Street and Third Avenue in Manhattan. That intersection was both a shopping center and the transfer point where commuters could board the Third Avenue El for a ride farther downtown. The horsecar service that was provided along Third Avenue in The Bronx to Fordham, however, was often unreliable. The cars ran so slowly that it was possible for passengers to hop off one as it passed by empty fields and pick huckleberries and then reboard the same car, even though it had continued to move. The horsecar route thus came to be known as the Huckleberry Line.

More people relied on the services of the railroad lines that connected The Bronx to Manhattan. It did not matter that the steam locomotive spewed forth ashes from the coal it burned for fuel, often soiling women's dresses and men's suits. The railroad was quick, and it got its passengers to their destinations on time. The railroad stations themselves were solidly built and were quite imposing. The one at Mott Haven was made of brick and sported a clock tower, while Woodlawn's station resembled a handsome country mansion with landscaped flower beds.

Most Bronxites were transported to Manhattan by the New York Central System. Its Hudson line served the wealthy residents of Riverdale. The Putnam division ran through spacious Van Cortlandt Park, providing service for people who wanted access to its magnificent recreational facilities. Its trains also brought the residents of Kingsbridge, University Heights, Morris Heights, and Highbridge over the Putnam Bridge crossing of the Harlem River to a terminal near the Polo Grounds in Manhattan, where they could take the Sixth and Ninth Avenue Els to get downtown. The New York and Harlem River Railroad, although administratively separate from the New York Central System, was operated by the same management and provided service to the villages along a central corridor of the borough, including Wakefield, Woodlawn, Fordham, Tremont, Morrisania, Melrose, and Mott Haven. The more sparsely settled eastern part of The Bronx was served by the

New York, New Haven and Hartford Railroad. In the summertime, its Bartow station, located in the middle of extensive Pelham Bay Park, would be crowded with pleasure seekers on their way to the shores of Long Island Sound. To get to City Island they had to transfer to a horsecar line, which took them to the City Island Bridge, where they would board another horsecar to get onto the island itself.

For Bronx residents the options available for travel would be greatly increased by a transportation explosion in the new century. The first system to be affected was the Third Avenue El. Initially, its northern terminus was at the very southernmost portion of The Bronx, at 132nd Street. Before the 1890s ended, however, extensions to the elevated railway were constructed and in stages the line advanced northward, first to 143rd Street and Third Avenue, and then along Third Avenue to 177th Street in 1891, to Fordham in 1901, and finally to Gun Hill Road in 1920. A branch was also extended to Freeman Street. These periodic extensions spurred building booms along the Third Avenue corridor.

At the same time, the old horsecars were gradually being replaced by trolley cars. Although the old horsecar terminus at 129th Street and Third Avenue was eventually eliminated, some of the trolley lines directly replaced the old horsecar routes. Indeed, the Third Avenue line continued to be popularly called the Huckleberry Line long after the plodding horsecar, which had inspired the name, had disappeared. After the routes of the new lines were determined, poles were erected along them to carry electrical wires that would provide power for the system. Tracks were then embedded in Belgian block (which most people called cobblestones), and frequent service was soon available. Passengers boarded the wooden trolley cars, sat in wicker seats, and paid their five-cent fare to the conductor. All the motorman was required to do was to make the car run. This system lasted until the manpower shortage caused by the First World War forced the elimination of the conductor. Free transfers between trolley lines enabled passengers to travel to the far reaches of The Bronx for a single fare.

The prime function of many of the new trolley car lines, especially those running east and west, was to connect passengers with the new subway lines, all of which generally ran north and south, to and from Manhattan. The subway was first extended into The Bronx in 1905, under 149th Street to Third Avenue. From that point, it was built in a generally northern direction, first as far as West Farms and Bronx Park, then to 238th Street, and finally to 241st Street and White Plains Road. When planning for the new line was taking place, there were comparatively few homes amid the wide spaces of fields and farmlands along the route. Since it was judged that no one would be particularly bothered by the rumble of rapid-transit trains running through such an open landscape, construction costs were kept down by erecting elevated tracks along the route and operating the subway trains over them. As had been the case when the Third Avenue El was completed, a building boom occurred, due not only to the new accessibility of living space in the city's northern borough, but also to the ease and convenience of inexpensive transportation to the heart of Manhattan. Apartment houses and shops were quickly erected within walking distance of the new elevated stations.

Other lines were soon constructed along elevated tracks in The Bronx. The Broadway subway was extended to Van Cortlandt Park, and the Lexington Avenue subway emerged from its underground tunnel between 149th and 161st streets to operate along Jerome Avenue, stretching first to Kingsbridge Road and then to Woodlawn Cemetery. A spur of the Lexington Avenue line was built in a tunnel under the built-up area of 138th Street, emerging after the Hunt's Point station as an elevated line, crossing the Bronx River to serve the farms of Soundview and the villages of Unionport and Westchester, and finally terminating at Pelham Bay Park.

Since so many of the new subway lines in The Bronx were elevated, it was not difficult for existing elevated lines to connect with them and to use the same tracks. This was true of the Third Avenue El at two different points. A spur of the El followed the tracks to Freeman Street, while the main line connected with the same elevated structure at a more northerly point at Gun Hill Road. Another convenient linkup occurred when the Putnam division of the New York Central abandoned the Putnam Bridge and its tracks were taken over by the Sixth and Ninth Avenue Els. A tunnel was then dug under the Highbridge hill, and the line continued as an elevated structure in the valley to the east, running just north of 162nd Street to connect with the Jerome Avenue line of the subway. The El trains then made their way north to a terminus at Burnside Avenue.

When the subway lines first began to operate in The Bronx, only shuttle service was available. No single train ran the entire length of the tracks from Manhattan to the northern part of the borough, and passengers going downtown were forced to change to through trains farther down the line. This provoked a popular outcry against the rapid-transit company operating the subway, and through service was soon provided.

The quick development of transportation in this period was made possible in large part by the use of electricity. With significant advances being made in technology, the Third Avenue El and most of the railroad lines were able to convert their operations from steam locomotion to clean, efficient electrical service soon after 1900. The advent of the electric age also led to at least two interesting experiments in passenger service in The Bronx.

The first one, and the longest lived was a high-speed commuter railroad that began operation in 1912. A subsidiary of the New Haven line, the New York, Westchester and Boston Railway was based at 180th Street and Morris Park Avenue. Despite its name, the line entered neither Manhattan nor Boston but served the sparse population of the eastern part of The Bronx north of its headquarters, while operating along the New Haven Railroad tracks south of it to 132nd Street. There, passengers could transfer to a spur of the Third Avenue El, which would shuttle them to the El's 129th Street station, where they could catch a through train downtown. The nuisance of transferring was mitigated in part by the speed of the new line and the comfort of its cars. Like trolleys, the cars were powered by overhead electrical wires, but they remained true railway carriages, with all the amenities. In addition, the stations, built especially for the line above 180th Street, were made of concrete and gave passengers the convenience of alighting on platforms rather than descending to ground level.

The second experiment was a monorail, which ran through Pelham Bay Park from 1910 to 1914. It consisted of a single car that ran along one rail on the ground and was supported from above by two rails held in place by an A-frame construction. Electricity was supplied through this overhead structure. Designed as a high-speed line to connect passengers exiting from the Bartow station of the New Haven line to the City Island Bridge, the monorail was badly hampered in its success by the reaction of the public to an unfortunate accident involving the tipping over of a crowded car on its initial run. Forced to keep its speed to a maximum of fifteen miles per hour, the line never received a full chance to operate at its best.

While most Bronxites preferred to travel by public transportation, a few had private means of getting about. Because physicians had to be highly mobile, many had their own horses and carriages to make housecalls. Similarly, the local grocer or pharmacist was expected to deliver packages to the fringes of the village and to the outlying farms, so most merchants had horses and wagons to do the job.

The century was less than a decade old when the first automobile made its appearance on Bronx streets. The loud whirring of its engine and the occasional backfires only made the machine a greater curiosity to the villagers. By the time of the First World War, several doctors had replaced the horse and carriage with the new contraption, and a number of the well-to-do could be seen riding about in models sporting a steam, electric, or internal combustion engine.

Although cars remained relatively scarce on Bronx streets during this period, the advent of the automobile helped to accelerate improvements that most Bronx residents had been demanding for years. The unpaved roads of the city's mainland borough were insufferable in the dry heat of summer, when breezes would raise small dust storms. In rainy weather, the same road would become an impassable quagmire of mud. Pavement had begun to be laid and sewers installed as early as the 1890s, but the first two decades of the new century brought the first serious renovation of the borough's thoroughfares. Streets were soon laid out across farmlands, the slopes of hills were changed to an easier grade, and angular or winding streets were straightened. Houses that had existed for decades beside the old dirt roads suddenly found themselves with their entrances now standing below the level of a raised street or high above on a regraded slope. Some houses in the path of a new or widened street were literally lifted off their foundations and moved to a new location nearby. When Fordham Road was widened, all the houses that lined the thoroughfare had their entrance steps moved a full ninety degrees. The Grand Concourse, a broad thoroughfare cut through an area that was mostly woods and farmland, bowed to the inevitability of the success of the automobile when its outer roadways were paved. The central section remained unpaved for those who wished to use their horses and carriages. To enable people to climb the steep slopes of escarpments in Spuyten Duyvil, Highbridge, and other places in the western half of The Bronx, there were constructed pedestrian streets consisting entirely of stairs.

The great improvement in transportation that made it easier for people to get around the borough was especially welcome in that there was also an increasing number of attractions for people to visit in The Bronx. Probably the first diversion to attract the residents of the mainland was horse racing. Trotting was very popular, and races could be seen at the Fleetwood racetrack north of the village of Melrose and west of the village of Morrisania. When new streets were laid out in the beginning of the century, Fleetwood closed, and its place was taken by the grid consisting of Sheridan, Sherman, and Grant avenues and their cross streets from 161st to 167th streets.

Those who disdained the trotters for the sport of thoroughbred racing had for many years spent their time at Jerome Park racetrack. When it was razed for the construction of the Jerome Park Reservoir, it was replaced in 1890 by the new Morris Park Racecourse on a site east of the Bronx River. The wealthy merchants and manufacturers of New York City would congregate in Morris Park on meet days, along with people from the surrounding villages, who were admitted onto the broad greensward for a day of picnicking to enjoy such races as the Belmont Stakes and the Eclipse Stakes. With the opening of Belmont Park in 1903, the thoroughbreds no longer used the Morris Park track, but in their place motorcar races thrilled the crowds, as did annual air shows which displayed the latest models of the new flying machines—even though some of the most handsome ones could not even fly. Such events were a regular feature of the course until a disastrous fire destroyed most of its Pompeiian-style buildings in 1910. The wind on that day was so great that some of the wooden structures in the village of Westchester to the southeast caught fire as well.

Another popular attraction at the time was of a more serious nature. When Henry Mitchell MacCracken built his New York University campus, he hoped to draw students with a colonnade that not only provided a spectacular view of the Harlem River valley but would also be used to honor distinguished Americans in a Hall of Fame. The Hall of Fame for Great Americans began operation in 1900 with the election of several people in various categories for the honor, each commemorated by a plaque affixed to the base of the colonnade. (It was not until years later that it was thought to place bronze portrait busts of the commemorated figures above their respective plaques in the spaces between the structure's columns.) While there was not really much for the visitor to the site to see, at the time it was the only Hall of Fame in the United States.

When Bronxites wanted to spend a day outdoors enjoying nature, they had a rich variety of options, for the area featured many fine parks. Most notable was the New York Zoological Garden (everyone called it The Bronx Zoo), which had opened before the old century ended. Here residents and visitors could view a herd of buffalo roaming the plains of Bronx Park, bears cavorting on the side of their own cliff, lions roaring in the lion house, monkeys swinging inside cages of the monkey house, and birds flying in a monstrous wire mesh cage.

North of the zoo was the New York Botanical Garden, which had been established only a few years earlier. The garden grounds were landscaped and planted to display different varieties of trees and flowers. An especially pleasant spot was a little wooden bridge just south of the waterfall in the park, near an old snuff mill that was now used for park business. The nearby Lorillard Mansion served as a police station until it was turned into a small museum. Early in the new century, a huge greenhouse, or conservatory, was built to house the plants of the rain forests and deserts—such as palms and cacti—that could not survive in the colder Bronx climate.

Local parks also provided many diversions. Frequent concerts were planned for Sundays and summer evenings. The Bronx's first playground was built in St. Mary's Park, an example that would soon be copied elsewhere in the borough. Van Cortlandt Park, especially, provided many an unusual diversion. At its southwestern end was the Parade Ground, designated for the use of the National Guard for training. Hundreds of people from the nearby villages of Kingsbridge and Riverdale would turn out to watch the Guard put on sham battles. When not used for military functions, the Parade Ground was used for polo games, and part of it was set aside for a cricket pitch where New Yorkers who had come from the West Indies could play the game. Adults who gloried in the sport of golf could use the links in Van Cortlandt Park, and many people came to row on the park's fine lake.

Other popular boating spots included the lake in Crotona Park and the Bronx River just below the zoo. Many enthusiasts went all the way to Tallapoosa Point in Pelham Bay Park to row a boat on Long Island Sound. Borough residents would even take the stagecoach to City Island, or get there via the Bartow station in Pelham Bay Park, for a day of sailing or for shore dinners at The Bronx's seaside resort. Despite its great distance from the other villages of The Bronx and the difficulty in getting there, the island would be filled with people on fine summer days. Some would go just to see J. P. Morgan's personal yacht.

Yachting was, in fact, a very popular sport among the wealthy. The Dodges of Riverdale had their own sailboat, which they moored at their dock on the Hudson River. The owners of mansions overlooking Long Island Sound all had yachts, except for Collis P. Huntington, who felt that he could travel every day on any of the many railroads he owned, but could use a yacht only six months out of the year.

Athletic events could be enjoyed by spectators throughout the borough. Before the elevated structure plunged it into perpetual shade, Jerome Avenue was a favorite place for marathon runners to train; inhabitants of the villages near the route would turn out to cheer on the participants when they ran the grueling race. Schoolchildren would hold their track meets in the Berkeley Oval at the southwest corner of Burnside and Sedgwick avenues. Local semiprofessional baseball teams used the athletic field of the Catholic Protectory at the southern outskirts of the village of Westchester, near the boundaries of Unionport.

In the hot, humid days of summer, boys would go swimming, often without benefit of bathing suits, in the upper reaches of the Bronx River or along the Harlem or East River. The sons of families who moved into Hunt's Point after the construction of the subway took advantage of a floating city facility that was anchored off the shore. This large wooden structure was built as a hollow square so that swimmers within could not be seen from the shoreline. Things were a bit more formal at Orchard Beach, the little resort that had grown up on Hunters Island in Pelham Bay Park. Here families owned tents with wooden floors. The tents were arranged in rows to form a miniature, if temporary, village for camping out during the summer. The nearby shoreline provided opportunity for bathing, though never, of course, without the full two-piece bathing suit.

In the wintertime, ice skating was the preferred sport. Every frozen lake would be filled with people gliding on the ice wearing skates clamped onto their shoes. While the lakes of Van Cortlandt and Crotona parks were the most popular with skaters, the tidal basin at the mouth of Cromwell's Creek was used as well, even though there was some danger that the salt water of the Harlem River could cause perilously thin ice. Unfortunately, landfill produced by the widening of the railroad cut for the New York Central in the vicinity of Mott Avenue was dumped in the basin, which was finally obliterated when Yankee Stadium was constructed on the site. The stadium itself opened with great fanfare in 1923. The New York Yankees, who had moved across the Harlem River from their previous home in the Polo Grounds, rewarded their fans with a world championship that year.

All these diversions became accessible to Bronx residents through the expansion of a successful public transportation network. While the immediate effects of this new system were beneficial, there were signs by the second decade of the twentieth century that the changes it was bringing were far more serious and wide-ranging than had been expected.

With the extension of the Third Avenue El to the northern reaches of the borough and the inception of the subway system, the sparsely populated region north of the Harlem River became ripe for development by real estate speculators. Because access to Manhattan was now easy and cheap for anyone residing in The Bronx, thousands of people poured out of crowded Manhattan tenements to make a new start in the country atmosphere of the city's mainland borough.

At the same time, Bronx residents who owned extensive tracts of land realized that the value of their property would be going up, and that their old way of life could not continue. Large landowners sold their farms and estates at about the same time that the new rapid-transit lines were under construction. Auctions of estates were numerous in the early years of the new century. The Ogden estate in Highbridge, the Varian farm in Norwood, and the Astor estate in Pelham Parkway all went under the gavel, and practically overnight the Simpsons, Tiffanys, and Foxes of Hunt's Point sold their property. In each case the land was divided into building lots, often for new apartment houses.

All these new structures were advertised by their landlords as "high class houses," a designation that usually meant only the wealthy could afford to live there, and there was initially some fear that the middle class would be driven out by the extensive construction. But in Hunt's Point, for example, apartment houses attracted large numbers of Jews from a working-class background, along with a substantial number of Irish and Italians. In general, the people who eventually did move into the four- or five-story walk-up apartments were just as middle class as the older residents of the area, and it was finally the fact that the newer inhabitants lived in rental housing that determined the major difference between the two groups.

The spread of apartment houses also meant the spread of local shops to service the neighborhood. Grocery, fish, vegetable, clothing, jewelry, and other stores opened, and a few thoroughfares became shopping streets. The first major shopping center in The Bronx grew up at the Hub, where Third Avenue and 149th Street crossed. The Hub's rise to prominence as a commercial area was rapid, as Bronxites quickly saw the convenience of changing their habits of shopping in major stores at 129th Street and Third Avenue in Manhattan and moving to shops at Third Avenue and 138th Street, and finally to the Hub. The Third Avenue El and the new trolley cars enabled people from all over The Bronx to travel to the department stores, furniture shops, and other specialty stores in the new commercial district.

This activity and growth, however, did disturb a number of longtime residents who sought to preserve a bit of the past that they considered valuable. Road building in Hunt's Point threatened the old Hunt family cemetery with destruction, but because the small plot contained the grave of Joseph Rodman Drake, an early American poet, a group of citizens under the leadership of Henry Mitchell MacCracken succeeded in converting the surrounding land into a park, preserving the gravesites for posterity. In another case, the growth of the village of Fordham threatened the safety of Edgar Allan Poe's cottage on Kingsbridge Road. A solution for its preservation was found in 1914, when the famous structure was moved to a new site in the northern section of Poe Park, across the street from the old location.

Unfortunately, not all such attempts met with success. Several informed citizens objected when the house of Gouverneur Morris was slated for destruction by the New York, New Haven and Hartford Railroad because it stood in the midst of its planned railyard in the southernmost section of The Bronx. The protest was too late. The house was destroyed, and the railyard was built.

A more significant disruption occurred when Europe was plunged into the First World War. The Bronx, with its large German ethnic population, was not at first necessarily sympathetic to the Allies. Yet when the United States declared war in 1917, National Guard groups formed to go "over there," and many a Bronx resident was called to the colors. At home, women hung little square pieces of white cloth bearing a blue star in their windows to signify that a man of the house was in the service. A great effort was made to raise money for each Liberty Bond drive. When the boys finally came marching home, a parade was held for them along Washington Avenue, The Bronx's traditional parade route.

But the war had been a turning point, and something had begun to change in the innocent world the people of The Bronx had known. One of the legacies of the war was a strong anti-German sentiment, so that it was no longer as respectable to claim to have come from German stock. A number of the old German gymnastic groups and singing societies disbanded. The rigors of prohibition also put an end to a number of German beer gardens. Most of the breweries in The Bronx either turned to making near beer or went out of business.

Prohibition was also a major blow to the Irish saloons. Despite the new laws, residents still demanded the right to drink, so a number of the old drinking establishments turned into speakeasies, where alcoholic beverages were sold illegally. Bronxites who had grown up learning to respect the law were now actively breaking it.

Other changes affected life after the war as well. A new morality seemed to grip the country. Women's dresses rose each year from a point above the ankle until, in 1925, they reached above the knee. Petticoats fell out of fashion and necklines plunged.

People from various parts of Manhattan continued to surge northward to new apartment houses along the subway lines. Since the 1890s, when they had been attracted by construction work for The Bronx Zoo, increasing numbers of Italians had come northward to live in the Belmont section. Other Italians settled in Melrose and in the northeastern part of the borough, where they felled the woodland to establish farms. Jews from the Lower East Side and East Harlem streamed into Hunt's Point, Morrisania and Tremont. Continued construction tended to obliterate the boundaries between villages, and the villages quickly became neighborhoods. Except for the northern and eastern fringes of The Bronx, where farms continued to exist, and except for the magnificent park system, which still gave a feeling of open space, The Bronx had become part of the city in fact as well as in name.

Although the period from 1890 to 1925 was characterized by dynamic change that transformed The Bronx from a suburban and rural district of farms and villages to an area of urban neighborhoods, there remained an air of innocence throughout these years. The people who moved to The Bronx were the upwardly mobile middle class of varied ethnic groups who came because they saw the borough as an improvement, a step up the social ladder. Their homes were neat, their relationships with others respectful, their business and economic transactions correct, and their children imbued with a set of values emphasizing duty, work, and charity.

Children growing up at the time looked at their world with wonder. The large fields, parklands, and empty lots where they played and let their imaginations roam were changed almost daily as a new subway was built or as a new apartment house rose. As the open spaces disappeared, the streets themselves became the play area. The children observed everything. They saw the stores, breweries, and factories of their neighborhoods, and the people who performed interesting jobs. They learned the discipline and curriculum of the schools. They experienced the flavor of living in a neighborhood in changing times when change was considered progress.

These children grew up and remembered their childhood fondly. Looking back at those times, they invariably saw them as more friendly and more civilized than The Bronx of their maturity. Some of them have recorded their recollections in articles for *The Bronx County Historical Society Journal.* Together, these memoirs paint a vivid and moving portrait of a Bronx that no longer exists, as well as providing an invaluable firsthand account of how The Bronx developed and how that process affected the neighborhoods and the people in them.

The issues in which many of these recollections first appeared are for the most part out of print. Their publication in this work will make them available to the public once again.

Enhancing and amplifying the narratives are over eighty photographs which chronicle the changes that occurred during these decades. They are chosen from the magnificent photographic collection of The Bronx County Historical Society's Theodore Kazimiroff Research Library, and in most instances, they are reproduced here for the first time. These photographs capture forever the changing scenes that characterized The Bronx in the innocent years.

MEMOIRS

Growing Up in The Bronx

WALTER PROPPER

Walter Propper, who grew up in The Bronx during the first decade of the twentieth century, describes some facts of life a child in the borough faced at that time. In an era of change and in an area of ethnic diversity, prejudice leading to racial and religious slurs did exist among children, but as Propper reminds us, it was not tolerated by the older generation, which tried to inculcate in the young a respect for all people.

The lower part of Prospect Avenue, where I spent my delinquent juvenility, was a side dirt road. Sixty years ago and across the street from where I lived, near 152nd Street, there was a large farm, the outskirts of which were considered the playground of the gang which included my brother and me. When we were hungry, or had nothing better to do, we swiped radishes and kohlrabi and other comestibles until the farmer threatened to physic us with red pepper loaded in a shotgun. I still do not know whether this treatment was practicable, but it sounded ominous and turned us to other forms of entertainment, like standing in front of a hand laundry on Westchester Avenue and yelling, "Chink! Chink! Chink!"

In those days the Chinese men wore their hair down their backs in long braided queues, pigtails, and they still clung to the pajama-like fashions of their native land. Our quarry, on this occasion, did not respond to our pleasantries with Oriental imperturbability but, instead, gave chase, and we, with our customary strategy, ran home to mother. My intrepid brother and I were less than track champions; we trailed the pack, and our pursuer, spurred by his indignation, was fleet enough to keep us in sight. We beat it through the alley and in the back door.

When, out of breath and with hesitant steps, we reached the parlor, our accuser, who had come in through the front door, was volubly, though brokenly, presenting his case to my mother. She beckoned me to the judgment seat and asked, "Did you?" I did not answer and she slapped me across the mouth and said, "Apologize." My brother fared no better. The plaintiff, his face saved, grinned amiably and we, who had been taught how to act on such felicitous occasions, offered our hands; and that was the way racial tolerance came to two young bigots.

Other lessons were not so easily absorbed. Nature, during the glacial age, had abundantly endowed our part of The Bronx with stones that made excellent missiles. As a result of this bounty a number of gangs sprang up in our neighborhood, and an undeveloped block on Kelly Street between Avenue St. John and Leggett Avenue became the area's battleground. Since the all-purpose weapon, the zip gun, had not yet been invented, it was easy enough to elude the enemy simply by keeping out of his range. But it was impossible to escape one's friends. Most of our casualties were caused by the bad aim of our own side, or when our projectiles fell far short of their mark. On the last adventure in which I was involved I, as usual, ran valorously home to mama with a scraped head. She compounded my misery by scolding, "I told you to keep away from those loafers." Some of those loafers later became lawyers and judges, teachers and engineers, and only one of them gained the distinction, so often predicted for all of us, of dying in the electric chair.

All of this happened over sixty years ago, just about the time that The Bronx became a county. In retrospect, the era of my delinquency seems to have ended then—and in a conflagration. The fire started out as an expression of patriotism, to celebrate election day, as I recall. Bonfires were common sights in those days; I remember that the people were always ready to pile up any kind of wood they could lay their hands on and light it just to see it burn. Six months prior to this election day we began to store barrels in our cellar. The whole block opposite to ours was then under construction with new tenement houses and we soon made a business deal with the night watchman, an inarticulate Russian with a predilection for beer.

The beer came out of our cellar. My father never kept an inventory of his beer reserves, and anyhow he was in the saloon and liquor business, which in a sense made the beer legal tender. For every bottle of beer that went out of the cellar, a barrel went in, a fair enough exchange, but something of a problem by volume. Thinking about it now, I doubt that my father ever realized that we were making a tinderbox of our home. What a bonfire that frame house and its ten neighbors would have made if an errant spark had gotten among those barrels!

The gang thought that it was engaged in a clandestine operation because most of the work was done at night when the watchman was on duty, but one day we were informed that the captain who commanded Engine Company No. 73, which was on the corner, wanted to see us. We were apprehensive, but not scared. All firehouses were staffed with good guys (probably still are, for all I know) and we were all assumed to be law-abiding people. The conference was not a pleasant one.

The captain was worried about the barrels in our cellar. He did not reveal much of what was on his mind, probably fearing to put dangerous thoughts into ours. But, in the end, he must have decided that he did not know of a better way to dispose of more than seventy wooden barrels than by burning them up, which, anyhow, would happen in about a week. In those days, when the population of The Bronx was between five and six hundred thousand, about one-third of the present number, and much more homogeneous than it is today, there was a rapport between the residents and the civil servants, and except for good reasons, no one would have disturbed it willingly. The barrels, and the potential danger which they represented, might, if a fuss had been made about them, have upset the serenity of the whole neighborhood. I know that if I had lived in one of those frame houses in our block and was aware of the barrels, I would have raised the roof until they were removed. But, apparently, the captain decided that he would worry through the few days before election and not interfere with our plans except to warn us not to increase our stock of tinder and otherwise to be very careful.

I am sure that our house at 643 Prospect Avenue was much on his mind during that week. Incidentally, it is no use looking for that address. Our house was not consumed in a Wagnerian pyre. It survived until a relatively few years ago, when it was razed and the land converted into a parking lot for a funeral parlor—which may have some Freudian significance.

In a way, the rest is anticlimactic. The fire came off on election day in good style, with the fire engine and the hose cart standing by in case of emergency. The engine, linked to the hydrant, pumped an operatic undertone to the conflagration and a line of hose stretched out toward the pyramid of barrels which some genius in our midst had caused to be erected. To me it seemed to be greater than the best they had to offer in Egypt. The whole neighborhood came to see the fire. Some lugged odds and ends of furniture which they wanted to get rid of. We all stood there gawking stupidly as the flames seemed to lick the clouds, and we inched backward as the heat became more intense. It took a couple of hours to reduce the pyramid to a smoldering ring of ashes and a few more minutes for the firemen to douse the last spark.

It took a little longer for my memory to put in proper perspective my awe of the awful energy which I had helped to let loose, and much later, I still had some pride in remembering that it needed a holocaust to turn a juvenile delinquent into a more or less solid citizen.

1969

Life in The Bronx: 1900

BERT SACK

Bert Sack recalls here the variety of sounds that were to be found on Bronx streets during the innocent years, as well as the tiring work that awaited the housewife every week.

There are thousands of volumes of history books, but few mark the everyday items that really make life and history. Here are some sundry notes on life in The Bronx not so long ago.

I recall some of the noises of everyday life which were all around us. I cannot forget the clanging of the old horse-drawn fire engine, its stack belching smoke and its shrieking whistle blowing louder than Gabriel's horn. There was the clang of the warning bells of the old trolley cars; other bells rang in a fast staccato as the trolley conductor counted the fares. The ragman's cart had its cowbells clanging along the street. Even our doctor had a little bell on the baseboard of his two-wheeled buggy, which cleared his way along the street when he stepped on it. The Bronx had its crescendo of sound at the Hub when the old steam locomotives of the El would whistle and ring their bells as they entered the 149th Street station. To this the chimes of the church at 151st Street and Melrose Avenue added their harmony. I remember the man who sharpened knives and mended umbrellas, carrying his grinder slung on his back and ringing his bell like an old town crier. The noise of the compressed-air drill today cutting into the bowels of The Bronx is but a whisper compared with the hammering of the old steam drills. I remember the horn of the fishman on Friday and the man who shouted "I cash clothes," the clippity-clop of the horse-drawn carriages and the chimes of churches which would fill the air for many blocks of wide-open spaces. I heard the bells of the convent in Hunt's Point at my home on Fox Street. One of the most famous of the old sounds, which lasted until World War I, was the German band with its big horn, playing Strauss waltzes and stirring marches, mostly out of tune. There were also backyard serenaders. The tenants would throw coins, sometimes wrapped in paper, down to them. Some of these sounds are still with us, but the congestion of the city has muffled them.

Electric washers, dryers, razors, low-heeled shoes, and lightweight clothes make life easy today, but what problems we had with clothes and other things in "the good old days." We had high button shoes and button hooks, high starched collars for men and the wire buttoner, detachable cuffs on shirts, and red flannel underwear. The underwear for ladies was not red, but just as heavy. We wore shaker socks, thick as a blanket, but they were warm on a cold day. The ladies were always in style, wearing their bustles to accent the posterior. "Rats" and "buns" placed beneath the hair were milady's aid to beauty. Everybody's grandma owned a "paisley" shawl. The men owned silver toothpicks and cigar cutters attached to their watch chains along with the big pocket watch. The ladies kept busy making "doodads" for the boudoir by crocheting around small fish bowls and test tubes.

Monday was washday, and that meant starch made with hot water stirred in the big dishpan and the homemade soap made with rendered fat saved for months and mixed with lye. It took out dirt and some of the skin of the person using it, as well. The end of the week was cleanup time in the home, and the kitchen stove was polished by mixing the shavings from a little black brick and water. Modern cleansers make work easy today, but then we had to scrape a big sandstone to get cleaning grit to clean pots and pans. We beat the dickens out of the carpets by using an old broom handle.

We had the old potbellied stove, red hot like the setting sun, and the stove's ever-present coal hood and shovel. At night we used smoky and dull "coal oil" (kerosene) lamps, and men wound up their day by relaxing in a smoking jacket and felt slippers. Those were the days—crude, maybe, but comfortable.

1966

ABOVE: Among the businesses located at the corner of Willis Avenue and 138th Street in 1907 is J. S. Diehl's book exchange, which is selling used and new books on the left. At 231 Willis Avenue is Paul F. Schnizler, sanitary plumber and gas fitter, displaying a new sink and toilet bowl in his window. He also sets and repairs furnaces, ranges, and heaters and paints and repairs roofs and leaders. After the narrow entrance to the apartment house is 233 Willis Avenue, the grocery store of Andrew Davey, selling butter for twenty-seven cents, three large cans of tomatoes for twenty-five cents, a package of rice for twelve cents, and a can of corn for six cents. If a person bought tea or coffee, he received free any article displayed in the window. Mr. Davey's horse and delivery wagon are parked at the curb. At the corner is Eckhoff's salon, which featured Eichler's Pilsener Beer.

BELOW: In 1909, the corner of 159th and Washington Avenue (here, looking north up Washington from 159th and Third Avenue) was a popular meeting place. To the right is the police station; to the left are frame and brick apartment houses with shops. A used-furniture company, stationery store, and carpenter's shop are the major businesses on the street. The delivery wagon for the Bronx Furniture Company can be seen awaiting an order.

RIGHT: A Labor Day celebration was held at Higgs Beach in Clason Point in 1911, the last year that the forty-six-star flag represented the nation. (In 1912, New Mexico and Arizona would join the Union.) The end-of-summer festivities were a time for Bronx families to enjoy good food and entertainment. Even the baby carriages were decorated with bunting and flowers.

ABOVE: At the junction of 149th Street and Melrose and Third avenues at the Hub in 1915, the subway kiosk in the center leads to the downtown IRT. The steel pillars to the right support the Third Avenue El above the street. Trolley tracks are in the Belgian block under the El and along Melrose Avenue behind the kiosk. A trolley car can be seen to the right of the elevated pillar, near the Immaculate Conception School. Shoppers could purchase men's suits at $10 and $15 and Mayfair women's shoes for $3. Services were even provided above street level, where the Melrose Dancing Academy taught dancing and a dentist promised to extract teeth without pain.

Kingsbridge at the Turn of the Century

GEORGE ARTHUR BERGEN

George Arthur Bergen recalls fondly the Kingsbridge of his youth, describing with great detail everyday life in a small village in the northwestern part of The Bronx. He refers here to streets by names that no longer are used. Ackerman Street is now taken up by the greater part of Corlear Avenue; Depot Place is West 230th Street; Church Street has been changed to Kingsbridge Avenue; and Water Street is now Corlear Avenue from 230th to 232nd streets. Webbers Lane has become West 232nd Street, while Cottage Row, a short street that ran from 230th Street almost to Albany Crescent west of Bailey Avenue, has disappeared.

I was born on October 31, 1893, at 12 Ackerman Street, village of Kingsbridge, just three blocks from the historic bridge. My paternal forefather was Hans Hansen Bergen, who was sent by the government of Holland to New Amsterdam in 1633 to promote improved methods of farming. Another forefather was Cornelius Berrien, a French Huguenot, who had to flee his native land in 1659 to New Amsterdam with his family for safety. My father, George W. Bergen, was born in the village of Westchester, now a part of The Bronx. He was the son of Nathaniel Bergen, a Bronx builder, and Mary Jane Berrien. At the age of nine, he went to live with his mother's sister, Margaret Elizabeth Berrien, the wife of Thomas Thorn, at Riverdale-on-Hudson, and was raised by them. My mother was Emily Miller from Naughton, England.

The era of the turn of the century properly falls within the last decade of the nineteenth century—which was known as the Gay Nineties—and the first decade of the twentieth century. I will describe the village of Kingsbridge as it appeared at that time within its boundaries. I will tell you what kind of people lived there and the lives they lived without the conveniences of today. I will tell you about their hardships and how they managed to overcome them. On the other hand, I will tell you about the joys they derived from the rugged lives they lived. I will explain what their yards and gardens were like, and then take you inside an average home. I will give you an idea of what the business section was like, and of the traveling tradesmen who made their rounds.

The people who inhabited the beautiful valley of Kingsbridge at the time were, on the whole, the descendants of early settlers from Holland and French Huguenots who had been compelled to leave their native country, with a large number of Anglo-Saxons. More recent arrivals were from Ireland and Germany. The children of these settlers were referred to as Irish-Americans and German-Americans. The children of these people were proud to call themselves Americans. All these people lived peacefully together as good neighbors. The newcomers pulled themselves up by their bootstraps, as it were, and managed to blend into the neighborhood. They were industrious, and soon owned their own homes.

Kingsbridge proper was located within the beautiful valley of Kingsbridge. This valley was bounded on the south by Marble Hill and the Harlem River to Fordham Road. The northern tip of Spuyten Duyvil Hill and the Riverdale woods bounded it on the west. It extended north to Van Cortlandt Park. On the east, it reached the tip of Kingsbridge Heights to border on Jerome Avenue. Broadway, which was then a dirt road, ran from north to south down the center of the valley. There was a horsecar which operated from the crossing of the New York Central and Hudson River Railroad north to the city line of Yonkers. The railroad ran through the lower portion of the village. It came up from the city on the east bank of the Harlem River and, after passing the grade crossing at Depot Place, started a long, sweeping half circle to the west. It crossed over Broadway and, entering a cut, passed under Church Street. Then, leaving the cut, it crossed Ackerman Street and the bridge over Tibbetts Brook and passed the last grade crossing over Riverdale Avenue. It then turned due south to the Spuyten Duyvil cut. The four grade crossings were manned night and day by rheumatic old gatemen. The gates were lowered and raised by the gatemen turning a crank on one of the gates. A warning bell signaled the approach of a train. On each side of the crossing were trestles to prevent track walking. Tibbetts Brook flowed south from Van Cortlandt Park, snaking its way through the lush salt meadows where pussy willows grew with an array of wildflowers. Meadowlarks and songbirds in the nearby Riverdale woods filled the air with a potpourri of sweet whistle melodies in spring, summer, and fall. There were not many streets west of Broadway due to the brook and meadows. They were Church Street, Ackerman Street, Water Street, and Riverdale Avenue, with Webbers Lane. East of Broadway there was Verveelen Place, Depot Place, Cottage Row, Bailey Avenue, Boston Road, Perot Street, Kingsbridge Terrace, Giles Place, Cannon Place, Fort Independence Street, and Sedgwick Avenue.

The homes were frame houses and cottages. They were fenced in and had gates. For the most part, they were privately owned and were painted various colors, with neighbors making sure they did not copy the colors of other homes. The yards and gardens were the pride of the owners. You could see well-kept lawns with flower

BERGEN
Kingsbridge at the Turn
of the Century

beds and gravel walks. Platform swings and hammocks were popular, as were rocking chairs for the porches. Most people had croquet sets. This was a popular game for both young and old. The reason people had their grounds carefully fenced in with gates was that during the dog days of August, you could expect a few mad dogs, frothing at the mouth, to come running through the streets until the police shot them.

The streets in the last decade of the nineteenth century were dirt. Men from the Corporation of New York would appear before election day and cut the weeds, rake and hoe the streets, and generally clean up. The sidewalks were paved with flagstones, and the gutters edged with flat stones. About 1897, they laid gas mains and set up lampposts. We liked to watch the lamplighters come running at dusk with their long poles with lighted wicks to turn on the gas and light the lamps. At daybreak, they would come running again to shut them off.

During the last decade of the nineteenth century, we had only kerosene lamps and candles. There were large, round, wicked lamps, with larger colored globes outside the regular globes. These were called Rochester lamps, and gave forth a steady, white light, which was excellent for reading.

The kitchens were the most lived in and popular rooms. They had running cold water with a sink. Behind the kitchens were the cellars. In these, the women stored products which did not require refrigeration. In each kitchen was a large icebox in which to store perishable foods. Charlie Acker, the iceman, knew when to come to replenish the ice. He wore a red flannel shirt and had a rubber pad on the left shoulder over which he carried a fifty-pound cake of ice with ice tongs. He carried an ice pick and would make the new block of ice fit by chopping away the old cake. Fifty pounds of ice cost ten cents. Each icebox had a drainpipe running down from the ice chamber. You had to keep a pan under the box to catch the water, and had to empty it on an average of twice a day during the hot weather.

In the kitchens were the cooking ranges. They used either wood or coal, or both. The women had large copper-bottomed boilers. Monday was washday. They heated up water and, with a knife, shaved in a quantity of brown soap and added a little kerosene to cut the dirt. They boiled the clothes and pushed them down into the water with an old broom handle. They had a second tub of hot water, in which they rinsed the clothes. Then came the job of wringing them out by hand. They were then placed in a wicker clothes basket to be carried out to the backyard, where they had heavy rustproof wire clothes lines at about six feet above the ground. On these, the clothes were hung to dry. It was a real sight to see all the clothes out on the lines all over the village on Mondays.

Tuesday was ironing day. Not having such a thing as permanent press, it was necessary to iron everything. This was a big job, and a hot job in hot weather.

On Wednesday, the women went social. They attended teas and card games, or visited with friends and relatives.

You may wonder how the women managed without telephones. You had three mail deliveries a day. The first was aimed at putting the *New York Times* on the breakfast table. This trip left the post office at about 7:00 A.M. The second left at 10:00 A.M., and the third and final at 3:00 P.M. A housewife could hand the carrier on the first trip a penny postal card, and it would be delivered to a friend or storekeeper on the second delivery. (Meats or groceries would be delivered that afternoon.) Eddy Martin was our letter carrier. I would see Pat Coleman leave in his horse and buggy to deliver to Riverdale. The others were foot carriers.

The housewives did not have to go to crowded stores and carry heavy packages home. They would be delivered on order. Another advantage was derived from traveling tradesmen. The man from the Great Atlantic and Pacific Tea Company would come in his red wagon selling tea and coffee. The tea and coffee were blended. If you gave a large order, you would get a free pot or pan. Gypsy tinkers came around in their colorful dress. While the men mended pots and pans, the women told fortunes. A scissors grinder would come down the street ringing his bell. He would sharpen scissors and knives. Then an umbrella man would come down the street, calling, "Umbrellas to mend." He would patch up, and put new ribs in, the damaged umbrellas. A milkman called daily. He sold loose milk at nine cents a quart. A pack peddler by the name of Herman made periodical calls. He sold dress goods, and would take orders for his next call. Charlie, the fishman, came on Fridays. He carried a zinc-lined bucket in which the fish were packed in ice. He had a small scale and a cleaning knife. When the shad was running in the North River, fishermen came with a wagon loaded with shad packed in ice. They would shout, "North River shad, three cents a pound." Peddlers came with wagonloads of fresh vegetables. In the spring, others came with wagonloads of flowers in pots ready for planting. Most all the women did their own baking. They sent to the bakery only when they ran short, or unexpected company called.

Food was purchased in bulk. My mother had the following stored in the cellar: a barrel of Pillsbury flour, a barrel of sugar, a barrel of Baldwin and a barrel of winter pippin apples, and two barrels of

BERGEN
Kingsbridge at the Turn
of the Century

sweet cider. When the cider became hard, my father sealed it to make cider vinegar. Mother put up all kinds of preserves, jams, and jellies. There was always a side of bacon hanging on a meat hook from which Father cut bacon for breakfast. The price of meat was very low as compared to the inflationary prices today. We ate well, and it was a standing custom in those days to give the children a dose of castor oil Friday nights to clean them out. After the winter was over, we all had to take sulfur and molasses or Hood's sarsaparilla to thin the blood. When school was out, and after they had changed from school clothes to play clothes, it was customary to see the children coming out with a large slice of homemade bread with homemade jelly spread on it. This was not only tasty but satisfying, and primed them for the games they played.

On Saturday nights, the traditional baths were taken. If any of you wonder why only once a week, then you should consider the work involved. Children were home on Saturdays, but the grownups had to work six days a week. There was no running hot water. The water had to be heated in the large copper-bottomed boilers. There were no bathrooms in the homes, and as the kitchens were the warmest rooms in the houses, the baths were taken there. We had large wooden bathtubs. The water was poured into two of these. One was for bathing and the other for rinsing off. In our bedrooms, we had large pitchers of water and, during the week, took sponge baths there.

I must now tell you about the rest of a typical home. The kitchens were the most-used rooms in the houses. Most of the time, we ate there. All of the cooking and baking was done there. We played games there and studied there. It was a living room in the true sense. We had a nice dining room on the second floor. The homes had dumbwaiters on which food was sent up to the dining rooms. Next to the dining rooms, and to the front of the houses, were the parlors. These were used for company and parties. Ours was nicely furnished with Victorian furniture. We had a good piano. Both my sisters played this, both solo and in duets. I played the violin, and we all played together. During the summer, when windows were open, neighbors who were listening would give us a round of applause. The bedrooms were on the third floor. Most homes had three, and some, four bedrooms. The parents would occupy the larger front bedroom. The children would occupy the others. In some cases, there was a spare room for guests. These rooms had good-sized walk-in clothes closets. There would be four-posters or iron bedsteads, and each bed had a nice feather mattress into which you could sink down on cold nights. The balance of the furniture consisted of a bureau, a washstand, and two chairs. The washstands had a towel rack on the back, three drawers to the left, and a cupboard on the right in which the chamber pot was stored.

On each washstand was a pitcher of water standing in a basin. Here is where you washed before going to work or school or to play. We all had sort of a combination saucer and cup with a finger loop for carrying, in which a candle was placed. These were kept in the kitchen and carried upstairs when going to bed. They were safe, and did not permit tallow to drop on the floors or stairs. Each bedroom had a small potbelly stove for use in cold winter nights. The windows were screened for summer.

As there were no toilets in the houses, the outhouses were in use. These unspeakable, but ever welcome, necessities were located in a far corner of the backyards, well concealed with vines, large flowers, and latticework. They had to be well insulated for cold weather. As a rule, there was more than one seat, with lower and smaller ones for the little tots. They were treated with lime, and once a year, men wearing rubber aprons and rubber gloves came around and, with big long-handled dippers, cleaned out the pits. The contents was poured into wooden casks with screw tops. These were carted away to no one knew where. I always felt sorry for these men, but the job they did was excellent, and there was no water pollution.

The business section of Kingsbridge at that time was located on Riverdale Avenue, which is now 230th Street. Riverdale Avenue started at Broadway and ran west around Godwin's Corner, crossed Church Street, Ackerman Street, and Water Street. When it came to the foot of Spuyten Duyvil Hill, it turned north and ascended to the Riverdale woods on a steep climb for one mile, and then continued to the Yonkers line. On the southwest corner of Broadway and Riverdale Avenue was a lunch wagon, which was operated by Mr. and Mrs. Rickendorf. Mrs. Rickendorf was a sort of rough woman. When a customer came to the counter, she would ask, "What will you have, beef stew or beef stew?" The customer would take beef stew. Then for dessert, there was a choice of apple pie or apple pie. The coffee was free.

On the southeast corner of Church Street and Riverdale Avenue was Larry Liebler's saloon, where weary men congregated after work to gossip and quench their thirsts. There was a family entrance through which the prudent could enter and, as they thought, leave without being seen. Here, you could buy a pail of draft beer for a dime.

Next to Liebler's on Church Street was Bobby Burns's shoe store. Bobby came to his store in a high hat and frock coat. You could buy a pair of Douglas shoes for a dollar.

Next door was the hand laundry run by Wong Lee. Wong only did men's shirts, collars, and underwear. He did an excellent job.

BERGEN
Kingsbridge at the Turn
of the Century

The last store before the bridge was the cobbler and shoemaker. It was operated by Tony, who stood well over six feet tall. It was said that he came from the north of Italy, where they grow taller.

On the north side of Spuyten Duyvil Creek from the bridge to Riverdale Avenue, and abutting Thorn's stables, was Fred Windler's grocery and vegetable store. The store extended from the bridge to Riverdale Avenue. In those good days, the grocers did not deal in pounds, like they do today. The dry measure was in use. You would not buy five or ten pounds of potatoes, for example, but a peck or a bushel of potatoes, and so on. Bananas were sold by the hand, cabbage and lettuce by the head, and beans by the quart. The only prepared cereals were cornflakes, shredded wheat, and Grape-Nuts, which sold at ten cents for a large box. There was a good variety of cereals that had to be cooked.

On the north side of Riverdale Avenue from Church Street to Ackerman Street was a row of stores with rooms upstairs. I was familiar with all the stores in Kingsbridge because, before I was sent to school, I ran errands for my mother and went to about every store on Church Street and Riverdale Avenue.

For meat, I was sent to Lew Schofield's butcher shop. Here you could buy meats from three cents a pound up to ten cents a pound for the best cuts. Soup bones and suet were free. A haslet cost ten cents, which consisted of the heart, the lungs, and the liver.

There was one barber shop run by Jake the barber. Here, you could get your hair cut for fifteen cents, and a shave was ten cents. There was a line of chairs against one wall and, across from the chairs, a line of cuspidors which Jake placed there to accommodate the tobacco chewers. Many of these were sharpshooters, but to the chagrin of Jake, a few missed the mark. Each man had his private shaving cup with his name on it and a picture. My father had a picture of a ship on his. I was anxious to grow up so I, too, could own my private shaving cup.

Over the barbershop was a free library. Miss Winn was the librarian, and was respected and liked by all.

Often, my mother sent me with a snip of cotton or silk to be matched at Stryker's notion store. I liked to go there and talk to the lovely Stryker sisters, who ran the store for their father. Hooks and eyes were widely used on women's dresses, and they had a large variety of these.

My mother, being English, drank a lot of tea. She blended her tea and coffee. I would be sent to Conklin's to buy a pound of Ceylon and a pound of Oolong tea, also a pound of Java and a pound of mocha coffee. The door to the store had a little bell which tinkled when you opened it. Charlotte Conklin would come out of the back room humming and say, "Now, where are my glasses?" We would say, "There they are, on your head, Mrs. Conklin." She would then say, "Oh, yes! So they are." To this day, I have always thought this was an act.

Then there was the confectionery. This was a popular store for the children. It was run by Mr. and Mrs. Geraghty and Mr. Geraghty's sister, Lizzie. Here, you could buy candy for one cent and a chocolate ice cream soda for a nickel. At Christmastime, Santa was sitting in the show window, showing toys to the children. We all thought that this was Lizzie.

Then there was Zurcher's bakery, which later became Hampy's.

We only had one doctor during the last decade of the nineteenth century, Dr. Parsons, who made his rounds in a horse and buggy. I remember his spotted carriage dog, which zigzagged under the buggy as the doctor drove along. The doctor was very busy, with more than he could handle. The villagers would have been at a loss had it not been for Mr. Hecht, our pharmacist, of whom it was said that he had been a doctor back in Germany. Dr. Parsons never complained when he sold counter prescriptions to people who came to him with their aches and pains.

Harry Berrien, who painted all the homes, ran a paint store on the northeast corner of Riverdale Avenue and Ackerman Street. When Harry was out painting houses, his daughter, Zelpher, attended to the store.

Across Ackerman Street, on the northwest corner, was Samuel Berrien's lumberyard and hardware store. Here, you could purchase the various kinds of building material needed and hardware articles for the home. My father told me that Samuel built most all the homes in Kingsbridge.

After Ackerman Street was Water or River Street. Both names were used. It faced Tibbetts Brook, with houses only on the side away from the brook. It was here that the tidewaters of the Spuyten Duyvil Creek met with the southerly flow of the brook. The people who lived here were plagued by flooding cellars, especially during neap tides.

West of this, on Riverdale Avenue, was Dave Power's plumbing shop. I remember Dave as a soft-spoken gentleman with red hair; his wife and all his children had red hair too.

After Dave's, you came to a shop I frequently visited. It was Mike Malone's blacksmith shop. I would spend hours watching Mike

BERGEN
Kingsbridge at the Turn
of the Century

shoe horses. As a special treat, he allowed me to work the bellows for him when he required extra heat. He shaped the white-hot shoes on an anvil, then dipped them in water. He filed the hooves of some horses, and if needed, would place a red-hot shoe on the hoof for a better fit. This worried me, and he said, "No, the hooves are like fingernails."

The last place of business on the north side of Riverdale Avenue was Patsey Stanton's plumbing shop. Patsey was a likable character. He had a sign on display in his office, which read, "If you spit on the floor at home, then spit on the floor here. We want you to feel at home." This sign seems to have brought the desired results. There were no tobacco stains on his office floor.

On the south side of Riverdale Avenue all the way from Fred Windler's grocery store to Spuyten Duyvil Road was the business of T. & W. Thorn and Company. They had coalbins under which wagons could drive to load coal. They had a large feed house where they stored hay straw and feed. They had piles of the larger grades of coal for schools, police stations, and other businesses. In all, they had forty-two horses and mules to pull twenty-one coal and feed wagons. Coal for homes sold for four dollars a ton during April, May, June, July, and August. After that, it was five dollars a ton. This was done to keep the men busy during the otherwise slack period.

A space within the open coalyards was rented to Dick Coffee. Dick ran a bottling works. This was another place I liked to visit, to watch Mr. Coffee filling bottles from a tub and then capping them. He carried flavors for root beer, cream soda, ginger ale, and sarsaparilla. He had been washing empties by putting shot in them and then filling them with water and putting them in a shaking machine. Patsey Stanton, seeing this, had rigged up a device with a rotating brush which would fit in the bottle, and, with running water, the bottles were cleaned in one-tenth the time previously taken. It was said that a flavor salesman, seeing this device, had it patented under his name.

There were many daily, weekly, monthly, and annual events which were part of the life of the village. People would gather to see the *Twentieth Century Limited* train go roaring by. They would wave to the passengers, who waved back.

Julia Morosini drove a handsome team of highly spirited horses in a sparkling-clean, shining carriage, with a coachman and footman decked out in livery uniforms. She left the Morosini estate, named Elmhurst, from Monday to Friday to meet the train which bore her banker father home. Each day, as they passed Ackerman Street on Riverdale Avenue, Mr. Morosini tossed out a handful of new pennies, and chuckled to see the scramble. The pennies were spent in Geraghty's for candy, with the ones lucky enough to pick up five treating themselves to a delicious chocolate ice cream soda. Julia, who was called Lady Bountiful, drove down in a green truck with Dave, the footman, before Christmas to hand out toys to the Kingsbridge children.

On Sundays, the stagecoach owned by William K. Vanderbilt would stop at the Kingsbridge Hotel for a rest and to change horses. With him he always had a bevy of pretty girls from New York's Four Hundred and some good-looking, well-dressed men. There was a trumpeter seated at the rear top of the coach, who frequently sounded the trumpet. For this reason, we called it the Tally-ho. At the hotel, they hitched a fifth lead horse on, ridden by a man whom we called a cock rider. This was done so that they could negotiate the steep climb up Riverdale Avenue.

Once a year, the Hoboken Turtle Club held a turtle dinner at the Kingsbridge Hotel. My father was a friend of the chef, and we always got a pail of delicious turtle soup. It was said that George Washington had been a member of this club.

Many socials were held in the parish halls of the Church of the Mediator and St. John's. The Mediator had a company of cadets and a marching band. It was a thrill to see them. At election time, there were night parades of Republicans and Democrats. As the streets were not lighted at that time, they carried red, white, and blue flame torches. In May, the girls made maypoles, and we went out on May parties. In the summer, hay rides were organized. The Fourth of July was a big holiday. Families vied with one another to see who could put on the best show. There were square dances, minstrel and other shows put on with home talent, and we enjoyed these more than professionals. The churches held strawberry festivals and card games, where women played euchre.

Boys up to seven years wore Lord Fauntleroy velvet suits, black stockings, and black button shoes. Over a fancy white blouse with lace collar and lace cuffs, a waist-length jacket was worn. Boys up to seven all had shoulder-length curls. Every morning, mothers wet them and set them and sat you on a stool until they were dry. The little girls were freer to play. The little boys were expected to keep clean. We could not leave our yards until we reached the age of five. One day, I watched two boys in the traditional dress engaged in a fistfight across the street from our house. The fight was fast and furious. They fought until exhausted. Then, cut and bruised, with curls and clothing disheveled, they shook hands and left. I was their unknown witness, and I wondered why they were fighting.

BERGEN
Kingsbridge at the Turn
of the Century

At the age of seven, the curls were cut off and stored in a box, and we were told to keep them. I still have mine. Then we were sent to Jake the barber for our first haircut. At seven, the boys all changed to knickerbocker suits, knee length, with belted jackets and peak caps. Black stockings came up over the knee and under the knickerbockers. The shoes were black and laced. The girls went into below-the-knee length dresses. They wore long hair down the back. Some wore it combed, and others, in braids or curls. The boys liked to dip the girls' braids into the inkwells at school.

From seven until sixteen, the dress did not change. Then the boys got their first suit with long pants, and the girls' dresses were let down to half-length below the knees. The girls then started to wear corsets and more petticoats. This was the age of parties and kissing games. "Sweet sixteen and never been kissed" was a saying, and the girls wanted to break that tradition. Women and girls wore dresses that buttoned or hooked up the back. They had to call on little sisters, or, as in my case, on little brother, to hook or button them. Some of the women wore bustles. To exaggerate the shoulders, the women wore leg-o'-mutton sleeves. Grown-up women's dresses swished and rustled as they moved about, and their skirts were of such length that men seldom saw their ankles. It was a real treat in those days when, on a rainy day, a woman had to hold her skirt up a little to cross a puddle and the men were treated to see the turn of her ankle.

Sunday was the day of rest. On this day, we all wore our Sunday best. We attended church at eleven, then read the Sunday newspapers, and after dinner the entire family went out for a walk. The men wore Prince Albert coats, gray striped trousers, derby hats, vests, watch chains, gloves, and canes. Boys seven and over wore derby hats and carried canes. The girls had lace collars, more petticoats, and fancier hats. The women added veils and larger hats and gloves. Their dresses were flared at the bottom. The women secured their hats with long pins, which, at times, proved to be a good defense in driving off a molester. They always had those little dainty lace handkerchiefs tucked up their left sleeve, which they sometimes used to take some dirt off faces, aided by a little spit. Many people drove in their carriages on Sunday. This, in dry seasons, was dusty. There was a bicycle path inside of the sidewalk on Broadway. There was a steady stream of these vehicles coming up from the city to the park on Sundays. There were single bikes, some built for two, and tandems in fours, sixes, and eights. At Van Cortlandt Park, you could hear a band concert, or watch polo games played by Squadron A against visiting teams. At times, there were military parades and sham battles. I recall one when they had soldiers dressed like the British redcoats and others dressed in the buff and blue of the colonial troops. The British came out of the woods to the north of the Parade Ground, and the colonial troops were lined across to the north of the mansion house. They used bugle calls and drummed. They used blank charges in their muskets and cannons. They cheered and charged, and many fell as if shot and were carried off the field of battle. It was exciting and almost real to watch, and I remember two being shown. At around 5:00 P.M., the people started for their homes, where they played music or read.

On weekdays, children of school age from Kingsbridge, Spuyten Duyvil (over the sixth grade), Marble Hill, and Riverdale attended Public School 7, Bronx, which was located on Church Street at Webbers Lane. The Singer estate, which cut Ackerman Street in two, provided the ground upon which the school was built. Before I attended, the principal was Mr. Davis, who ran the school military style. He had a drum and bugle corps, and sounded colors at 8:00 A.M. to hoist the Stars and Stripes, and a bugle call to summon students to class. Students formed into class companies and marched to class. My two older sisters were in school before Mr. Davis left. When I went to school, Isaac B. Sprague was the principal. The teachers taught the "three Rs," Reading, 'Riting, and 'Rithmetic. They drummed the times tables into us and gave us a really good grounding for high school. They maintained discipline with the ruler and the pointer. We were made to write with the right hand, and reading started in the first grade. The Reverend Tieck has published a book on the schools,* so I will not say any more about them.

After school, and on Saturdays, we played games out of doors. The girls did a lot of rope skipping, singing different verses as they skipped. They played hopscotch and jacks. They played Red Rover with the boys, and a game called Tap on the Back.

After school we played many out-of-door games. We went into the woods and cut our hockey sticks. With this, we played shinny on the street with an old tin can. For shin guards, we cut out parts of old bamboo shades. In the winter, we played hockey on Tibbetts Brook. These were rough games.

There was one called cat. The bats for this were cut from old broom handles. The cat was made from a piece of the handle about two inches long. This was sharpened at one end. A six-foot circle was drawn on the ground. The cat was placed in the center of the ring. Like baseball, we had boys in the field. However, there was but one base. Two men would be in to bat. The cat was

---

*William A. Tieck, *Schools and School Days in Riverdale, Kingsbridge, Spuyten Duyvil: The History of Public Education in the Northwest Bronx* (Old Tappan, N.J.: Fleming H. Revell Co., 1971).

BERGEN
Kingsbridge at the Turn
of the Century

hit out. If it was caught in the air, the batter was out. He had to make first base. If time permitted, he could run home and score a run. Otherwise, the other man would have to bat him in. If that man was caught out, then a player from the field would come in. This man could bat in the man on first. This was a rotating game.

As we did not have enough players to form two baseball teams, we played baseball by what was called all around one. The game would start with all positions in the field covered. The rest of the players were in, ready to bat. The rotation was from batting to left field, right field, center field, third base, second base, first base, shortstop, pitcher, catcher, and then up to bat.

We did a lot of swimming in the summer. To get to the swimming hole, we had to hold our arms up and run through a clover field full of honeybees. I only heard of one boy getting stung.

We made canoes and bows and arrows. We made our own kites, and, in the winter, made skis from barrel staves.

We did a lot of fishing. The girls were good at catching blue-clawed crabs. They tied a piece of beef on a string, and with a scap net in one hand, would scoop the crab in. They had to be adept at this, and fast.

In winter, we floated downstream on ice cakes. I fell in one time. The water was so cold that I could hardly get my breath, and my clothing froze on me as I ran home to change.

Hares and Hounds was a great game. We had to appoint a gamemaster. We played this in the Riverdale woods, and ranged for about two square miles. The hares were given twenty minutes to start. Every time they changed direction, they had to leave a clue. The hounds had to trace them by these clues. If the hounds spied the hares, they could chase them direct. The hares had to get back to home base to be safe.

We also played Duck on the Rock.

For diversion, we would catch some garter snakes and chase the girls with them. The girls would scream and run away. We never got too near them with the snakes. Yet, after we walked away, the girls would come back to be chased again.

Sleigh riding was a great sport in winter. We were blessed with a mile-and-one-half run down Riverdale Avenue. Families built elaborate bobsleds. They used the cane seats from old streetcars. They fashioned a steering rod. They had foot rests for the riders. They were big, and held fourteen people. These bobs would race down Riverdale Avenue at breakneck speeds. It only took two minutes to make the mile-and-a-half run, but it took a half hour to haul the bob back to Barney's Gates, the starting place. No one could ever beat my cousin Bill Stewart's bob. The kids with sleds, cutters, and Flexible Flyers would let the bobs go first, and then all would go belly-woppers down after them.

There were snowball fights between the boys on Ackerman Street and Church Street. Church Street had a lot of boys from large families, like the Seelers and Reeves. Ackerman Street had the greatest number of boys of any street in Kingsbridge, and could take them all on. We had the Gross boys, the Martins, the Flanagans, the Morrisons, the Lynches, the Murrays, and the Jarzenskys. These were the boys I was brought up with. Many were good friends for life. Mr. Martin let us use a shed he had as a club. There, we had a punching bag and boxing gloves, which were in use daily.

When winter was over, it was time for spring cleaning. This was a big yearly job. Carpets had to be taken up, and the carpets and rugs taken out and hung over the clotheslines. With rattan carpet beaters, the dust had to be beaten out of them. For this work, it was necessary to wear bandannas over your hair and a wet cloth over the nose and mouth. Saturday was the usual day for this work. All the windows had to be washed inside and window screens dusted, washed, and painted.

At times, there would be two boys who wanted to have it out with a fistfight. Such fights were held at about 7:00 P.M. on Saturdays. There would be a referee, and the rules of the fight were known as Queensberry. There were no timed rounds. The fight went to a finish. Most all the boys at that time were skilled boxers. Every one of those fights which I saw ended in draws. After the fight, the boys shook hands. I never heard of anyone being knocked out or seriously hurt. The use of knives or pistols was unheard of. Everything was settled by bare fists in a fair fight.

At the end of the baseball season came a big event. The teams of the Church of the Mediator and St. John's played. There was a lot of feeling behind these games, and the turnout of fans for each side was always great. There was one game I will always remember. At the bottom of the ninth inning, the score was Mediator 7, St. John's 6. There were two men on base, with two men out and two strikes on the batter. The St. John's fans had all lined up and were shouting and jeering and trying to disconcert the Mediator pitcher, Tony Shook. I do not know whether it was this or not, but the batter slugged out a hot liner which brought in two runs, and St. John's won by one run. At this moment,

BERGEN
Kingsbridge at the Turn
of the Century

Burney McGinn, the St. John's catcher, and Jim Connors, the catcher for the Mediator, jumped at one another and engaged in a fistfight, which was promptly stopped by spectators. However, another fight started. Rex, a dog owned by the new pastor of St. John's, Father Kelly, and Prince, the dog owned by Dr. Campbell, the rector of the Mediator, had it out. Prince won, so the Mediator fans went home with a feeling that all was not lost.

Early in 1900, electricity was introduced. Electric streetlights were installed, and the gas lampposts were taken down. Gas water heaters were being put in the homes, with running hot water. Along with this, bathrooms were built in the homes. The Saturday night bath soon became just a bad dream. These were good things; but there was another thing that happened during the progress of the first decade of the twentieth century, which set things back.

On the night of October 27, 1903, a fire started in Thorn's hay, straw, and feed building. The cause was never settled, and there were many different opinions. It was a windy night, with the wind coming from the west, which was just right to cause the most damage. My father rushed out to supervise the saving of the horses and mules. A year previous to the fire, my mother had insisted that the outside doors be installed to each stall in case of fire. It was this foresight that saved the horses and mules. The fire raged out of control for a long time, notwithstanding the valiant fight put up by the firemen. Three-fourths of the business section was wiped out. We were all stunned. The losses were great, and some never recovered from it. With what they had left, business resumed. Zurcher's sold out to Hampy from Tremont. Otherwise, the same owners remained. The businesses completely wiped out were T. & W. Thorn and Company, Fred Windler's grocery, Harry Berrien's paint shop, Sam Berrien's lumberyard and hardware, Dick Coffee's bottling works, Dave Power's plumbing shop, Mike Malone's blacksmith shop, and Patsey Stanton's plumbing shop. T. & W. Thorn and Company built a new yard at 215th Street and the Harlem River. A feeling of sadness settled over the people of Kingsbridge. They knew things would never be the same again.

In 1905, Cleveland E. Dodge founded a new public library situated between the Mediator and St. John's on Kingsbridge Avenue, the new name for Church Street. The great and beautiful elm trees remained still to beautify the scene.

In 1906, the New York Central started to use the new shortcut which had been built on the north side of the Harlem River Ship Canal. The four grade crossings were eliminated, and the cut became a walking shortcut to Broadway. That big half circle became a thing of the past.

Kingsbridge at the turn of the century was a paradise of beauty, never to be forgotten. The people who lived there at the turn of the century were the best one could ever wish to associate with. They lived out their lives in this snug and beautiful valley, content with what they had earned by honest hard work. I would gladly exchange all of today's conveniences for those glorious days when we had so little and, yet, so much.

1976

Street Scenes

At Melrose Avenue and 162nd Street, looking north in 1899, are walk-up apartment houses on the right and frame houses to the left and center. A bakery, a meat market, and a dry goods store occupy the buildings' street level. Beyond the homes at the head of the street lie the tracks of the Port Morris and Spuyten Duyvil Railway. The two houses facing Melrose Avenue would later be removed to build a bridge over the railroad tracks, connecting Melrose to Webster Avenue on the opposite side.

ABOVE: Broadway just south of Mosholu Avenue was an almost deserted road for carriage traffic in 1899. The Mosholu Hotel, at the left, catered to travelers and to those who wished to refresh themselves in its indoor café or outdoor pavilions. The empty lots immediately to the left of the hotel are for sale. To the right is ten-year-old Van Cortlandt Park. Mosholu Avenue was extended through the park, and at the Broadway intersection stands a sign directing riders to Riverdale, to the left, and to Woodlawn, to the right. Trolley tracks can be seen on either side of Broadway.

BELOW: This view of Johnson Avenue and West 228th Street circa 1900 is dominated by the Johnson Avenue wall. At the center of the photograph, a policeman on horseback is climbing the hill. The small house beside Spuyten Duyvil Creek could be reached by a footbridge.

A grassy mall occupied the center of Prospect Avenue as it stretched southward from the Longwood Avenue station of the elevated subway that ran along Westchester Avenue. In 1909, the taxpayer to the right housed, at street level, an elegant restaurant, Wolffberg's Infants' and Childrens' Wear store, and the Cosmopolitan Bank, and a dentist's office and amusement facility in the story above. Beer barrels are placed around the telephone pole on the sidewalk in front of the restaurant. Across the street, at the street level of the neighboring five-story brick apartment houses bearing limestone trim, are Halper Brothers' Pharmacy, a laundry, a real estate and insurance office, and a store in which soda was sold. In the street in front of the neighboring five-story brick apartment houses, a horse-drawn wagon from the firm of Cording and Saltzmann, headquartered at 135th Street and the Harlem River, is tipping back to deliver a shipment of coal. A wooden church stands on the next corner. Trees have been planted recently on the sidewalks near the curbs.

A view of east 180th Street north
on Boston Road circa 1910 shows
the entrance of the Bronx Zoo in
the distance. The boathouse on the
Bronx River is to the right rear.
The approach to the zoo passes in
front of Tietjen's saloon. A sign
behind the saloon advertises the
Lyon & Chabot department store at
the 149th Street Hub and urges
visitors to the zoo to dine at the
Rocking Stone restaurant.

ABOVE: From Westchester Avenue at Westchester Square, looking northwest in 1910, one can see the stores on East Tremont Avenue. Among them are the Knickerbocker Market, the Westchester News Company, a saloon, a theater, a confectionery, a restaurant, Peterson's drugstore, and a grocery. The horse trough and drinking fountain in the center of the photograph were donated by a Mr. Cooley.

LEFT: At the intersection of Third Avenue and Boston Road in 1912, Boston Road, with its Belgian block pavement, rises to the right, flanked by walk-up apartment buildings and street-level shops. The apartment house to the left has four- and five-room apartments, all with light, bath, and hot water, at low rents. The box beside the streetlamp to the left is for the temporary storage of mail for the postman to pick up and deliver on his rounds, while the small box attached to the pole in the center was used by people to mail their letters.

ABOVE: On November 6, 1913, Perry Avenue near 205th Street had already been paved for two years. Substantial frame houses flanked a quiet tree-lined street where children played. One of the early automobiles in The Bronx is parked along the curb.

Fordham Road looking east at Tiebout Avenue on February 10, 1914, shows a quiet scene with recently planted trees. A five-story brick walk-up apartment house stands to the right and frame houses and shops in the center, including P. J. O'Reilly's grocery store and L. Wolf's meat market.

Bailey Avenue just north of 231st Street was a tranquil spot in 1915. Only a delivery wagon and a lone horse occupy the street. Farmland covers the area to the left above the point where Albany Crescent enters Bailey Avenue. Across the street to the right, new "high class" brick houses with five-room apartments have been built near older frame dwellings.

Haffen's Brewery

SALLY STEINBERG

Sally Steinberg had the unique experience of living close to one of the borough's major establishments—the Haffen Brewery. From her vantage point she could observe how the beer was bottled and distributed. The childhood of a girl growing up at that time in the village of Melrose was filled with many joys.

Returning to the scene of one's childhood is an uncanny experience. Haffen's Brewery, which occupied the corner of Melrose Avenue and 152nd Street and ran up 152nd Street at least halfway, was gone. The street, seen through adult eyes, seemed to have shrunk. However, the house I had lived in as a child was still there.

In 1913, my father moved his family of seven children into a yellow frame house opposite the Haffen brewery. He had purchased the rights to the bottling and distributing of Haffen's beer. Pipes ran underground between the brewery and a large shop on the ground floor of our house. Rubber pipes were inserted into bottles to fill them and then they were capped and labeled. In the shop, there were hand-operated capping machines and two large washtubs for washing the bottles piled at the rear of the shop. The place was permeated by a damp, sharp odor.

Behind the shop was a cobblestoned yard and a stable in which horses were kept. They were large "beer" horses, and on Sunday a rather frightening treat was to be seated astride one of them for a ride around the yard. My youngest brother, Jimmie, and I were both seated on one horse (with our legs sticking straight out on each side) and the horse would be led to and fro across the yard.

It was a sad, rainy night when one of the drivers came to the house to report that Willie, our favorite horse, had slipped and broken his leg and was killed. Jimmie and I left the room to bawl on each other's shoulders.

Next to the entrance to the shop was a door leading to our living quarters. One flight up there were three bedrooms, and a small sitting room which we called the "library" because it contained more books than anything else, in addition to a leather and mahogany living room set and an organ. The organ had to be pumped with pedals and that would mean enlisting the aid of one of my brothers when I wanted to play it. My legs could not reach.

The large bedroom at the rear of the house was occupied by my parents. There was a potbellied stove there which offered the only heat on that floor. We would get into our nightclothes in front of it and run to bed. The beds were warmed up with beer bottles filled with hot water. In the middle of the night we would push them out of bed. They had turned cold.

This floor also contained a second bathroom (an unheard-of luxury), which was equipped like a country outhouse. The top floor had a fully equipped bathroom, a very large kitchen with a coal-burning stove, a large dining room, and another bedroom.

Through the window of my parents' bedroom, on the lower floor, we would climb onto the roof which covered the shop below. It was a wonderful place for playing and raising flowers.

On the corner of 152nd Street and Melrose Avenue, there was a circular stoop, which we called "Haffen's Beach." Mr. Haffen's office was located at the top of this stoop, and when the office was closed, the children of the neighborhood would gather there.

Mr. Haffen would leave his office at the end of the day in a chauffeur-driven auto, and we would all stand around to watch the car tilt to one side when he stepped inside it. Mr. Haffen enjoyed his own product. He would invite my father in every afternoon to sample the newest brew and indulge in German conversation.

When Mr. Haffen died and his son inherited the brewery, he closed it down completely. This was a tragic situation for the adults, but not for the children. My father got rid of the horses and we had another place to play in. The stable was a wonderful place for playing hide-and-seek. We'd hide in the hay and sometimes a mouse would run over our ankles and we would give away our hiding place.

To the right of the building, in the rear, there was an archway and a shed for storing the wagons. My brothers hung a swing on chains in this archway and gave each other what they called a Coney Island ride. After you were seated, the chains were twisted tightly and then released, and you would spin around very quickly. The one time I tried it I could not retain any food for a day. I was forbidden to go on again.

We lived in many homes after the yellow house, some of them more modern and nicer and in better neighborhoods, but none are recalled with the nostalgia of "Haffen's Beach."

1976

Recollections of Riverdale

CLEVELAND E. DODGE

Cleveland E. Dodge reveals for us the world of the wealthy estate owners in Riverdale in the early years of the twentieth century. In addition to being the heir to the family's Phelps Dodge copper interests, Dodge inherited the family's charitable undertakings, some of which he discloses here. Remarkably, except for his acquaintance with Mark Twain and his family's possession of a yacht, his reminiscences are not much different from those of others residing elsewhere in The Bronx at the time.

My grandfather, William E. Dodge, Jr., bought some land from Major Joseph Delafield about 1859 and built a stone house, which was completed in 1863. The architect was James Renwick, an Englishman, who was also the architect for St. Patrick's Cathedral on Fifth Avenue. As the history of the Delafield property is interesting, I will give a brief account of it. Major Joseph Delafield was an officer in the Engineer Corps of the U.S. Army. Along with several other men, he served on the commission that surveyed and determined the international line between Canada and the United States all along the St. Lawrence River. Another project of which the Major was placed in charge was building the forts on either side of the Narrows between Brooklyn and Staten Island. In those days, slag lime was used for mortar for bricks and stonemasonry. Major Delafield, therefore, searched for a place where he could quarry limestone and found a satisfactory deposit several hundred feet above the Hudson River on land just above what is now Palisade Avenue. A small kiln was built to produce slag lime and a rock dock built on the river where sloops could tie up to receive shipments of slag lime for the forts. At that time, in the early 1830s, what is now Canal Street in lower Manhattan was being made by filling up an old canal. Major Delafield purchased one of the tollhouses, which he moved to Riverdale for a house for the foreman of the lime quarry. This house was on my grandfather's place for many years and was used by one of his gardeners. Unfortunately, a few years ago, through the carelessness of a Park Department employee, it burned down.

Apparently in those early days deer and wild turkey were common in the area. A large piece of property was owned by a farmer named Hadley, who lived in a house on the Post Road that was built about 1765 or earlier. When Major Delafield became familiar with the place, the farmer was in debt and forced to sell his holdings, which stretched from the Hudson all the way to the old

Post Road at Van Cortlandt Park. Major Delafield purchased the property, which was mostly woodland, with only a small portion suitable for agriculture. A few years later, he built a small house for a vacation place. This house, after a good many changes, is still in use just across 246th Street from the Jewish temple, in Ploughman's Bush.

Riverdale was originally part of Westchester County, before it was engulfed by the greater city. Up until early in the century, it was mostly a summer resort with perhaps twenty-five private places scattered along the slope facing the Hudson River. People traveled back and forth to the city on the New York Central, which had steam locomotives, but made about the same time between Grand Central and Riverdale station as is the case today. My family had a house in the Murray Hill district, but spent summers and most weekends in winter at Riverdale, where my parents had built a brick house on former Delafield property adjoining my grandparents'.

There were really only two small settlements in the area at that time. Here, a few tradespeople and men working on the private places lived. Many of these people were Irish and on the whole there was a contented atmosphere and friendly feeling in the community.

So when I was a young boy and teenager, Riverdale was only sparsely settled. Except for our place, all the way from the Hudson River to the Post Road at Van Cortlandt Park, there were undeveloped woods. My brother and my two sisters and I had a big Saint Bernard dog and our parents felt that it was safe for us to wander around all over the neighborhood. As we grew older, we had ponies to ride and drive. The family kept cows for fresh milk and kept up a chicken yard and vegetable garden. During the First World War, my mother kept sheep on the lawn. We had better ponds in the Delafield woods and on the Goodrich place, where the children in the neighborhood played hockey on the ice. There was good coasting on what was the Pyne Hill, which was afterward purchased by Dr. Jerome Webster. Skiing was just becoming fairly common, but up to that time, no proper shoes and straps were in use. We just had toe straps, which were no good for making curves.

There were no definite dividing lines between Spuyten Duyvil on the south and Ludlow and Yonkers to the north. In Spuyten Duyvil, the Johnson family were the most important. They owned the iron foundry and a good deal of land. There were, however, a number of smaller residences too. In Riverdale, well-known names included James Scrimser, William A. Butler, Waldo Hutchins, Percy R. Pyne, T. R. Hollister, H. F. Spalding, Robert Colgate,

D. W. James, S. D. Babcock, James Bettner, W. L. Morris, Frederick Goodrich, and a number of others, including the Delafields, who held by far the largest acreage.

Gradually houses changed hands to new owners, and many of the larger places were partially subdivided. Many of the new residents were interesting people. One of these was General Webb, who was a Civil War hero and later became the president of the College of the City of New York. When I was a boy, he had a long white beard and was a great favorite of all my family. Another well-known man was Darwin P. Kingsley, president of the New York Life Insurance Company. He drew others from his company to settle in Riverdale, including Thomas A. Buckner, who succeeded Kingsley as president of the insurance company, and George W. Perkins, who left a position with that company to become a partner in J. P. Morgan & Company. Mr. Perkins was a strong backer of Theodore Roosevelt and the Bull Moose party, but especially endeared himself to people on the Hudson River by saving the Palisades and developing Bear Mountain Park. Besides Mark Twain, we much later had Toscanini and Professor Bashford Dean of Columbia University, who rented the Wave Hill house from Mr. Perkins and had a well-known collection of armor. At another time, the British government leased Wave Hill for their ambassador to the United Nations, Sir Pierson Dixon. During his residence there, the Queen Mother, Queen Elizabeth, paid an official visit to New York and stayed with the Dixons. My wife and I were included in a small reception for Queen Elizabeth. The guests were divided in groups of about half a dozen persons, and the Queen moved from one group to another, talking to each for ten minutes. She was very simple and cordial and made a great hit with everyone. She was also very kind in giving the children of neighbors an opportunity to shake hands and talk with her.

Before the Henry Hudson Parkway was constructed, Riverdale Avenue was just a fairly narrow road. Until about 1909 or 1910, there were very few automobiles and most of the wealthier people kept horses and carriages, with sleighs for the winter. The most fashionable sleighs were driven by Miss Julia Morosini, who had several sets of white and red harness and reins and beautiful fur rugs.

There was a saloon, known as Jumbo's, at the corner of Riverdale Avenue and 254th Street. It was a favorite social spot for coachmen, since the beer was good, resulting in horses stopping there automatically. Later, the place was purchased by George W. Perkins and my father, and was presented to the neighborhood as a house for a visiting nurse and a place to meet for Boy Scouts and various organizations. This eventually grew into the Riverdale

Neighborhood House, which was built on Mosholu Avenue and was occupied in 1937.

To the south of our place was the Delafield property, and to the north, part of the original Pyne place, which was developed as Alderbrook. The next place to the north belonged to George W. Perkins; it later was given to the city and is now operated by Wave Hill. To protect his own property and garden, Mr. Perkins bought the adjoining Wave Hill place, which was built by W. L. Morris and, when I was a boy, was owned by William H. Appleton, head of the well-known publishing company. After Mr. Appleton's wife died, the house was rented to Mark Twain and afterward was sold to Mr. Perkins. The Clemens's youngest daughter was just about the age of my sisters, and as she wanted company, she spent most of her time in summer at our house. Mark Twain loved children and became a good friend of our family. He was just as picturesque and interesting as he has always been described. I have met a number of authors who were disappointing although I like their books. Old Mark was even better than his books. One morning I went to his house with a message and found him receiving mail at his door from the postman. He was chuckling over one letter addressed to "Mark Twain, God Knows Where." He gave my mother a photograph of himself with the inscription: "Truth is the most valuable thing that we have, let us economize it."

My father was very fond of sailing and always had a yacht, the last one a large schooner which he kept at City Island. He had a dock on the river at the foot of our place and, when a young man, used to take our whole family rowing in an extra-large-sized Adirondack boat. He bought a fifteen-foot sailboat, which my brother and I sailed almost every day in summer. The lower part of the Hudson is not usually a good place to sail, as the tide runs about four miles an hour and the sides are high, with the Palisades on the west and high banks on the east. There were lots of boats on the river in those days, especially long tows, two-masted line steamers. We used to steer our small sailboat as close as possible to the steamers so that the boat would get caught in swirls at their sterns, which would twist our boat in circles. We had many picnics on the Palisades, which were fun to climb around and beautiful with the vertical overhanging cliffs.

In those days, a quarry company was opening directly across from Riverdale. The quarry produced traprock, excellent for railroad ballast, roads, and foundations for buildings. Very heavy blasts were used, so that the broken rock slid right down into the scows on the river. My father and other neighbors succeeded in getting Mr. Perkins to promote the Interstate Park Commission, which condemned and saved the face of the Palisades. Mr. Perkins also was successful in persuading E. H. Harriman to turn over his property to the commission. This property became Bear Mountain Park. Later, John D. Rockefeller, Jr., quietly acquired a strip of land all along the top of the Palisades, which saved that area from being built over by ugly buildings.

Father's generation swam in the river, but when my sisters, my brother, and myself came along, the Hudson had become pretty polluted. Father built a thirty-foot egg-shaped swimming pool near the house, which as far as he could find out was the first out-of-doors pool in the United States.

There was a firehouse on Riverdale Avenue, which was later rebuilt, but at the same location as the old wooden building. The equipment was horse-drawn. There was an upper story with room for the men on duty. For speedy action, in case of an alarm, there were brass poles to slide down to the ground floor. The older children and I used to love to go there to see the horses and were allowed to slide down the poles, which was exciting since the upper floor was a long way above the ground.

There were no real stores or shopping district until much later, after I had finished college. My family purchased from a grocery and market on Riverdale Avenue in south Yonkers. The best shops for other things were at Getty Square in the center of Yonkers. My mother had an early type of telephone attached to the wall in the pantry. Receiving orders on the phone, the stores would make deliveries at the house. The ice problem was solved by an ice wagon coming when needed, with big square chunks of ice for the refrigerator. Originally, our house was lighted by gas and oil lamps, but it was not long before electricity was introduced in the neighborhood.

When I was a child, my father bought a fine Shetland pony, which lived until I grew up. We had a two-wheel cart and would drive all over the district, including the Speedway, now the Harlem River Drive. We used to race men with fast trotting horses and could keep up with the best of them.

Riverdale started to change gradually when automobiles became common. This led to the Delafields' developing their big property between Riverdale Avenue and Broadway into the restricted residential area of Fieldston. Fine houses were gradually erected and, early in the development, Mr. Hackett started the Riverdale Country School. Not long afterward, Teachers College built the Horace Mann School for a practice and demonstration school for student teachers.

The radical change in the neighborhood came with the building of the Henry Hudson Bridge and Parkway in 1936, along with new subways that provided an easy access to the downtown city and led to apartment houses, paved streets, and shopping centers. In spite of all that, the district has retained a great deal of friendly community feeling, due largely to all the work and interest of a great many volunteers, who work hard and effectively. So much of the area has been zoned for one-family houses that it has done much to keep pure air and not too much crowding. We hope now the land already owned by the city, along with the intervening area, will be kept for a greenbelt, which would further help in retaining trees and some open spaces.

1975

Parks

In 1901, the New York Botanical
Garden was under construction.
A young student from nearby
Fordham Prep stands in front
of the recently completed
Conservatory. *(Courtesy of Fordham
University Archives)*

The New York Botanical Garden's Conservatory and Museum Building lie across Southern Boulevard from the farm at St. John's College, Fordham, seen here in 1901. Like other Bronx farms, the college facility raised fruits and vegetables, but the produce was solely for the use of the students, faculty, and clergy at St. John's. The farm remained in operation until the First World War. *(Courtesy of Fordham University Archives)*

ABOVE: The parade ground in Van Cortlandt Park, circa 1909, was the site of the games and races of Squadron A of the New York State National Guard. Vault Hill, which held the remains of the Van Cortlandt family, rises in the background.

RIGHT: The Bronx Zoo obtained animals from all over the world. In 1923, a truck convoy returns to the zoo from the pier with its precious cargo. The truck in the lead is carrying a supply of fodder for the animals. The initials on the door and below the license plate stand for New York Zoological Park.

LEFT: The Bronx Zoo provided for its visitors an ice cream parlor, seen here in 1915. A customer would pay for his soda in advance at the cash register and receive a soda check in return. He would then give his order for any one of twelve flavors of ice cream soda, or for White Rock ginger ale or Kola Ade, to the attendant at the fountain, and he could drink it seated on a bentwood chair. Cigars, popcorn, and picture postcards of the zoo and its animals were also available from the cash register attendant.

I Remember Tremont: 1911–1918

GEORGE DIAMOND

George Diamond describes here, with remarkable vividness, the bustling commercial world of Tremont in his youth. Here can be seen The Bronx in transition from the old rural village, with its feed store and county fair, to the crowded commercial street packed with shops of all kinds, where people of all ethnic groups did their marketing. Mr. Diamond and his friends grew up in the midst of this activity, playing in empty lots and along the tracks of the New York Central Railroad.

In 1911, my father moved his pet shop from 111th Street and Third Avenue, in Harlem, to Tremont and Park avenues, in The Bronx. At that time, Tremont Avenue, from Webster to Third avenues, was one of the main business streets of The Bronx.

There were two bars, one on each corner of Tremont and Webster. One had a restaurant behind it, where my father used to pay the cook to save scraps for the dogs. Downstairs, it also had a poolroom and a bowling alley. Many a Saturday night I worked as a pinboy in the bowling alley until about twelve o'clock, mostly for tips.

The bar on the opposite side of the street had swinging doors in front. Kids used to swing on the doors and cry, "Is my father in there?" The bartender would then scream out, "Get off those swinging doors."

Many a time my father would send me for ten cents' worth of beer and the bartender would fill the pail up to the top. Since I had to carry it back with me, he told me to be very careful and try not to spill the beer. I used to fill my pockets with pretzels while he filled the can.

Further up the street was Richard Webber's, a general store, where you could buy almost anything in the way of food and groceries, meat and vegetables. Here was a preview of what the future supermarkets would be like: everything under one roof. My father was friends with the German butcher there. The day after Thanksgiving, he watched the butcher pack the turkeys in ice to put into the icehouse. He then explained to my father that this was the second year he was putting them back and that they were still called spring turkeys.

A little further up the block was Bloom's house furnishings, with all kinds of gifts for the home. The glassware and china were packed in straw and I used to go there to pick up the straw for the rabbits' cages.

Then there was Bartell, the florist. He used to have a greenhouse about a mile long along the Bronx River below Gun Hill Road.

On the corner of Tremont and Park Avenue was a large warehouse called Santini. This property later became what is today the Eastern Savings Bank.

Around 1912, the New York Central used to run local all the way down to 125th Street, and from there, express down to Grand Central. The subway only came up to 149th Street, and there you got the Third Avenue El to Fordham Road.

Since my father had his pet shop on Tremont and Park avenues, the New York Central was my playground. My friends were a League of Nations. Tommy McKean was Irish; Jack Rose was English; Amelia Screvoni was half Italian and his mother was a Southerner (when I went to his house alone, his mother used to say, "You all sit down to eat," and I would look around to see if there was anyone else there); Jim White was a colored boy; George Vitarius was a Greek; and an Armenian boy was called Artemus.

Next to the lot was a feed store where you could buy all kinds of feed for horses, chickens, ducks, geese, or other livestock. Next to the feed store was Dr. Amster, a veterinarian.

There was also Shipman's stationery store and, a little further down, Schwartz's clothing for men and Glaser Brothers ladies' and children's wearing apparel on the corner. One flight above, there was an Italian restaurant. When you sat down, they would place a coffeepot at your elbow for a starter and follow it up with wine.

On the corner of Washington Avenue, there was an ice cream parlor where you would take your girl for an ice cream soda. Also at that intersection was a Rexall drugstore. They often used to run a penny sale. If you bought one item, you could get a second similar one for a penny.

A little further down Tremont Avenue, there was a large clock high up on a metal stand near the curb. It always had the correct time. There was also a water trough, where horses could drink their fill.

There was also a coffee and tea store. Here you could buy loose tea from many different parts of the world. Coffee came in large burlap bags. Most people had their own coffee-grinding machines, but if you asked the proprietor of the store, he would grind the coffee beans for you in his coffee grinder, which had two big wheels on the sides.

There was also a tobacco store, where you could buy loose tobacco for your pipe or to roll your own cigarettes. Bull Durham used to sell little bags of tobacco with cigarette papers.

There was also a cigar store with a wooden Indian in front of it, where cigars were made out of clean Havana tobacco leaf. They would roll the tobacco and put it in wooden frames to get a shape. Today, they use dyed paper instead of tobacco leaf. The workmen were given a certain amount of tobacco, from which each had to make one hundred cigars. Whatever was left over belonged to them. My father's friend worked there, and he used to sell my father one hundred Havana cigars for three dollars. In the back room of the cigar store, men used to play pinochle for cigars, the losers having to pay.

Around the corner on Washington Avenue was the Tremont post office, and the next building was the Tremont Methodist Church. Opposite the post office was St. Joseph's Church, which had a large steeple on which lived a pair of pigeon hawks. You would often see them with a pigeon in their claws, which they would devour. Next door was a Woolworth five-and-ten-cent store, which also had an entrance on Tremont Avenue. At that time, nothing in the store cost more than a dime. Today, the dime does not even pay the tax.

There was a bridge over the New York Central tracks, and one of the games we played was follow-the-leader. Each time one of the boys used to do something spectacular, every one of us had to follow him. Over the tracks, there were girders supporting the bridge. One of the kids squeezed inside a girder and shimmied down to the roof of the station below, keeping his hands over his head. Then I tried it, but I had something in my pocket and I got stuck inside the girder. I thought I would never get out of there. Finally, my friends pulled me up by my arms. I think if our mothers had seen us doing such terrible stunts, they would have fainted.

Our game of tag was a hair-raiser. We would run up and down the railroad tracks.

We would also climb from the top of the station onto the pipes which ran along the wall about twelve feet above the tracks, until we came to a spot where we could get off.

We had a clubhouse under the stairway bridge going over the tracks near 174th Street. At one time when we were there,

there was quite a bit of excitement. A woman jumped off the bridge right in front of an oncoming train and she was killed instantly.

There was also a pole supported by three cables, which boys would climb, causing the pole to swing back and forth. While doing so, they sang "Sailing, Sailing, Over the Bounding Main." Once, when I was swinging on it, all of a sudden I heard a crack and I went sailing down to the ground with the pole. I let go when the pole was almost near the ground, and, landing on a piece of angle iron, fractured my foot.

At that time, the New York Central's station on the south side of Tremont and Park avenues had a Western Union office. In those days, sending a telegram was the fastest and most practical way to communicate. The telegrams were delivered by foot and bicycle. There was no such thing as airmail. Western Union was pretty busy at that time and you could always see the rack with many bicycles in the front, coming and going all day long. The messengers were called "mutts." You could even wire money by Western Union at that time. Now there are no messengers: everything is done by phone.

On the southeast corner of Tremont and Park avenues was Woodall Real Estate, where you could have bought acreage very, very cheap all over The Bronx: farms, woods, and private houses with large plots of land.

Next to the real estate office on Park Avenue was a very old barber from Europe. Every customer had his own cup and shaving brush. My father had a shaving cup with his name printed in gold. I used to think my father was very important to have his name on a cup. The barber used to boast that he was Napoleon Bonaparte's barber when he was a young fellow.

There was an empty lot on the northeast corner of Tremont and Park avenues. One day, I was playing in the lot, fell down, and got a nail right through my finger. My mother almost fainted when she saw it, but she took good care of my finger and it healed nicely. Later, Fox's Crotona movie house was built where the lot was.

Near Bathgate Avenue was Polly Preston, shoes for women. On the corner of Bathgate was Wartell, the jeweler. Around the corner was the police station. Across from the police station was Fox, the undertaker. Next to the police station was St. Joseph's Church. On the next block was Unger, the pawnbroker, with the three balls hanging over his door. Once, my friend woke him up at two o'clock in the morning to ask him the time. Unger said to him, "What's the idea of waking me up to ask the time?" He said, "You have my watch."

A story was going around at that time about a man who bought a gun in the pawnshop and held up Wartell, the jeweler. The cops caught him and took him to the police station. He escaped and ran across the street, where the cops shot him in front of Fox, the undertaker. A service was held in St. Joseph's Church and Fox buried him.

Sometimes my mother used to take me along when she went shopping on Bathgate Avenue. At Trackinberg's delicatessen, on 174th Street between Washington and Bathgate avenues, you could get a frankfurter and sauerkraut for ten cents, or a corned beef club sandwich with coleslaw or potato salad and a piece of pickle for the very low price of twenty-five cents. At times, my mother would buy a large pickled tongue for one dollar.

People came from far and near to shop on Bathgate Avenue. As you turned into Bathgate, you saw the stands in front of the stores and the pushcarts in the gutter. The stands and the pushcarts were loaded with fruits, vegetables, clothes, goodies, toys, pots, pans, dishes, false teeth, eyeglasses, and more.

There was a large bakery where you could get large, freshly baked rolls with moon seeds, onion pretzels, bagels, or soft rolls, for ten cents a dozen. Bread was eight cents a pound, with or without kimmel seeds. Large egg kuchels sold for two cents each. Loose milk was also sold in the bakery, at seven cents a quart. It was ladled out with a quart dipper from a large milk can which had big chunks of ice in it to keep the milk cold. Even with the ice in it, the milk was much more creamy than today's milk, since it was not pasteurized or homogenized in those days.

A little further down was a kosher butcher shop, where my mother usually shopped. The butcher would cut a piece of meat from the whole chuck for twenty-five cents a pound. There were no special cuts at that time. He could give my mother plenty of free bones for the soup she would make with the meat. For another two cents, he would give my mother the miltz and lung, from which she used to make fricassee.

On the fruit and vegetable stands, the fresh items would be piled up in the front, but the salesmen would give you some of the stuff from the back, so that when you got home you would find rotten stuff in the bottom of the bag.

In those days all commodities were quite cheap. Eggs were selling at fifteen for twenty-five cents. If you found a bad egg, you could return it and get another one. Butter sold for twenty-five cents a pound.

You could buy almost anything in Bathgate. Near Wendover Avenue (now Claremont Parkway) there was a live-chicken market where you could always buy a freshly killed chicken. You could buy loose dried prunes, pears, apricots, and cherries to cook for dessert or to make into Wishnick brandy.

At the appetizing stand, my mother used to buy dill pickles at one cent each, or small green tomatoes for the same price. Sauerkraut was sold by the pound, if you brought your own jar. My mother would buy a large piece of lox of about two pounds or so, for about twenty-five cents a pound. She would make slices from the center of the lox for everyday snacks and meals. The rest she would cut up in cubes and pickle. Also, she would buy smoked butterfish, carp, kippered lox, and smoked carp, all for twenty-five cents a pound. Sturgeon and baked salmon cost a little more. Delicious halvah was sold by the pound, for twenty-five cents. It was kept in a box and sliced. There were barrels of schmaltz herrings in front of the stand. Some sold for five cents each, and some for eight cents each. Some, a trifle larger, were ten cents each. There were also barrels of pickled herrings, marinated herrings, and matjes herrings.

There was a fish stand with all kinds of fresh fish, including live carp, where you could pick out the one you wanted from the large tank where they swam around. You could also buy fresh fish from a wagon in your own neighborhood.

On Bathgate Avenue, a little below Tremont, there was a large building where they held county fairs, and where you could buy homemade pies and cakes, fresh honey, all kinds of homemade jams and preserves, fresh buttermilk, and homemade cheese. Everything was fresh.

Fagerson's hardware store was there. Around election time, one flight over the store there would be a moving picture machine. Across the way would be a picture screen. They would flash election returns on the screen as they came in. They would also show a Charlie Chaplin or Ben Turpin picture and some advertising. The streets would be jammed with people watching election returns.

On Third Avenue near Tremont was Dominick's Clam and Oyster Bar. We used to get an oyster sandwich with two large oysters for fifteen cents. It was right near the exit of the Third Avenue Elevated, and at night, before people came home, they used to stop there. The Third Avenue El was the main source of transportation at that time in that area.

On Tremont and Third was the United Cigar Store, where they would give out coupons which looked like real money, although they were smaller in size. Later, the doughboys passed them off in France for real money. Some of the cigarettes, which were sold in flat boxes, were called Helmers, Fatimas, Mecca, Egyptian, Deity, Salome, and Turkish Trophies. Then there were different brands of pipe tobacco. Dill's Best sliced pipe tobacco, which came in slices and which you crinkled up and put in your pipe, came in flat tin boxes. Also there were Rum and Honey and Prince Albert for the pipe smokers. Many brands of chewing tobacco came in packages; some came in plugs from which a piece could be bitten off. There were also little in-between cigars which came in small, flat tin boxes.

There was also a ladies' millinery shop where women could buy custom-made hats. A woman would try on many a hat until she found one to fit her face. Some hats had small brims, some had large brims, some had feathers or flowers. There was quite a choice.

Also, there was a large fruit store owned by my friend's father. At Christmastime, he had the whole sidewalk covered with Christmas trees. My friend used to drill holes in the trees and insert surplus branches into them so that he could get more for the trees.

There was a moving picture studio on Wendover Avenue near Park Avenue. If you were willing to stand in line for a few hours, you might get a job in the moving pictures. You would get two dollars to be in a mob scene. Sometimes they would rent pets from my father's store to put in a picture. Once, I went to the studio with a parrot. It was a picture with Theda Bara. The actors and actresses had a lot of makeup on their faces so that they could photograph better. I had to wait for the parrot and take it home when they got through with it.

The triangle of land from Tremont Avenue to 178th Street between Webster and Valentine avenues was all closed in by a billboard fence. We kids made a hole under the fence where we could climb in. There were thick woods inside, with bushes and trees. Surprisingly, we found a peach tree, loaded down with nice, large peaches. We used to gobble them down when they got ripe.

The Tremont movie house was across the street from the billboard fence on Webster Avenue. They showed silent pictures with a piano accompaniment. When a picture was sad, they played sad music. When horses were going fast, they played fast music.

Sometimes they would have a singer at the Tremont, and while he sang, they would show slides on the screen. They would show an apple orchard and a girl on a swing while he sang "I'll Be with You in Apple Blossom Time."

The Tremont Mills, where I had my first job, was on Webster Avenue and Ittner Place. Today, the Cross Bronx Expressway goes through that area. There were all kinds of ribbons manufactured at the Tremont Mills. Ribbons were used for bows on the hair, sashes on dresses, for trimming slips, underwear, hats, and many other things. My salary was six dollars a week, four dollars of which I gave to my mother. I felt like a rich man, as I did not have to ask my father for spending money.

On 175th Street and Webster Avenue there was a blacksmith shop. Once in a while the blacksmith used to give me a penny to deliver a horse to the stable for him. When I said OK, he would lift me up onto the horse's back and slap the horse. The horse would start to run and I would hold on to the mane for dear life, as he had no saddle or bridle to hold on to. The horse would run into the stable on Park Avenue and I was glad to get rid of him. The stableman once asked me to take another horse back to the blacksmith, and I said, "Nope."

Next to the blacksmith was Kramer's live-chicken market. My father would buy Rhode Island Red or Plymouth Rock chickens from him to sell in his pet shop. Lots of people had chickens in their backyards. Across from the chicken market was a stable where we used to rent a horse-drawn surrey with the fringe on top to go to Van Cortlandt Park for a picnic with the whole family. Next to the stable was Boker's restaurant, where you could get a good breakfast consisting of ham and eggs, toast and coffee, for thirty-five cents.

On 175th Street and Washington Avenue was a corner saloon where my friend Amelia Screvoni's father used to play a mandolin, accompanied by an old man with a harp. People used to give them money for entertaining them. The old man had snow white hair and looked like Father Time. He lived with the Screvonis and used to carry the harp to the saloon on his back.

Across the way from the saloon was the huge gas tank. This was where gas was manufactured. Natural gas was not used at that time. My father used to buy big bags of coke there for burning. Coal was very scarce and more expensive for heating and cooking. Coke was derived from coal from which most of the gases had been removed by heating. It weighed about half as much as coal and burned very fast.

On 176th Street and Webster Avenue was a rental laundry, which rented out uniforms by the week to restaurants, butchers, and other places. On the next corner was a lumberyard. Next to it was Bartell, a wholesale glazier, who installed storefront windows and sold all kinds of glass.

The firehouse was on 176th Street near Park Avenue. The firemen used to hang out in the barbershop on Park near the southeast corner of Tremont Avenue. They worked twelve hours a day at that time. They used to train the horses every day by backing them up into the fire truck in teams of three. The harnesses were hung up on the ceiling with ropes on pulleys which could be lowered down on top of the horses in a few seconds. When the fire bell would ring in the firehouse, you could see the firemen come sliding down the pole, back the horses into the fire trucks, and harness the horses, all in a matter of minutes. Out they would come with the clang, clang, and smoke and fire coming out of the fire engine, and the hook and ladder, with a fireman in the back, steering the back wheels. The firemen on the running board would be pulling the string which rang the bell on the fire truck. Last but not least, the white dog with the black spots would run after the fire engine. And all the people would run into the firehouse and ask the man in charge where the fire was.

Borden's milk company was on Park Avenue near 180th Street. They had a big stable where you could see the big wagons with teams of horses bringing in the huge cans of milk from the railroad. At that time, milk was delivered to the homes by horse and wagon. The milkman would carry the quart milk bottles in a metal frame. He would walk from one floor to another, leaving quarts of milk at the door of the customer. He would also pick up the empties. People would leave notes in the bottles telling the milkman what they wanted. Sometimes he would walk to the top floor and find a note to leave an extra bottle of milk or a bottle of cream. When he came down, the horse and wagon would be waiting at the next stop. The milkman had to keep a book with records of how much milk and dairy products were delivered to the people. Once a week, he would collect the money owed to him. My mother was told by her doctor to drink plenty of sweet cream. My father used to walk over to the Borden company and buy three quarts of returned milk which was brought back by the drivers. He would spill off the sweet cream into his pail. Out of three bottles, he would have one quart of sweet cream.

A few of the places I mentioned are still standing. Most of them are now memories of Tremont.

1974

Business and Industry

James Stephens & Son coal company had its headquarters at 138th Street and the Mott Haven Canal. In this photograph, taken circa 1900, a canal boat is docked next to the company offices, while a horse-drawn coal cart is crossing the wooden bridge over the canal.

The sign on the structure supporting the bridge's cables reads: "$5.00 Fine for Driving Over this Bridge Faster than A Walk." Note how unpaved 138th Street has been turned to mud by a recent rainfall.

ABOVE: In 1909, the Edison Studio at Decatur Avenue and Oliver Place was a center of motion-picture production. Famed director Edwin S. Porter filmed some of his photoplays for Thomas Alva Edison's company here. The glass-walled structure on the left, with its high ceiling, provided plentiful light for the shooting stage. The street had not yet been paved. *(Courtesy of The Astoria Motion Picture & Television Foundation)*

RIGHT: Southern Boulevard at 145th Street, circa 1910, was a center for the manufacture of pianos. To the right is the factory of Decker & Son, at the center is Ernest Piano Company and C. Brambach & Son Pianos, and farther to the left is the Berry-Wood Piano Player Company. A saloon in the center of the photograph served thirsty workers at closing time. Suspended from the trolley wires is a sign indicating that the intersection is a school stop.

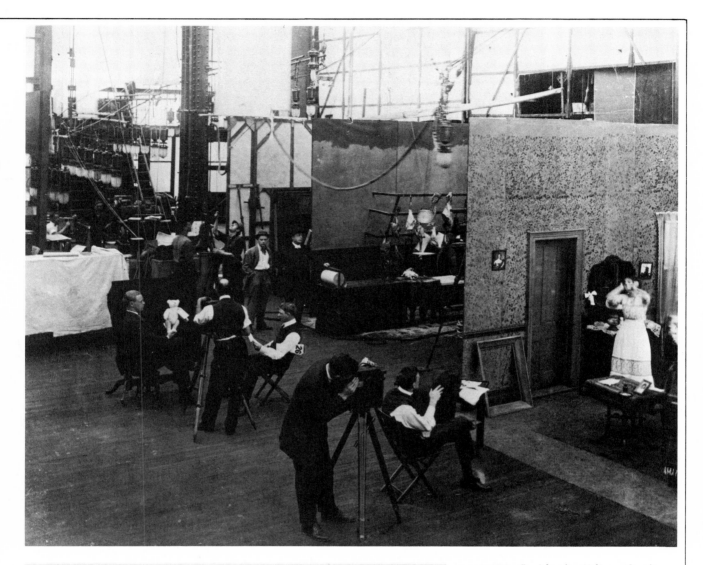

ABOVE: Inside the Edison Studio in 1912, an actress is being directed to emote on a set showing a typical bedroom of the period. Next to her, a set for a butcher shop awaits use, while technicians adjust the scenery and the lights. Shooting a movie amid such cacophony was possible because the films carried no sound track. *(Courtesy of The Astoria Motion Picture & Television Foundation)*

RIGHT: Inside the Biograph
Studios in 1919, the director,
Robert Z. Leonard, and crew of
the film *Miracle of Love* discuss
possible camera angles, while
carpenters, painters, and other
craftsmen build the set. Above, a
skylight admits natural light.
*(Courtesy of The Astoria Motion
Picture & Television Foundation)*

ABOVE: In 1912, the Biograph
Studios on 175th Street near
Marmion Avenue housed one of
the major motion-picture
companies of the era. Here, famed
director D. W. Griffith shot the
interior scenes for his last Biograph
film, *Judith of Bethulia*. *(Courtesy of
The Astoria Motion Picture &
Television Foundation)*

The Smith and Haffen Building stood at the intersection of 148th Street and Third and Willis avenues. Looking south in 1908, Willis Avenue is to the left, while the 149th Street station of the Third Avenue El can be seen to the right. The Smith and Haffen was one of the first office buildings erected in The Bronx. It housed the Knickerbocker Trust Company, the Home Life Insurance Company, and a real estate office.

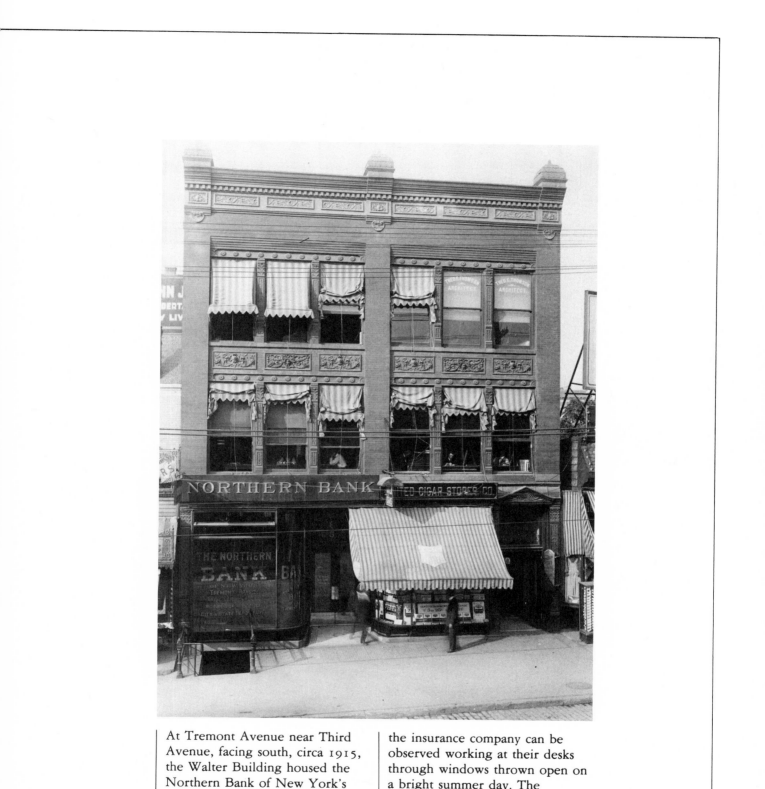

At Tremont Avenue near Third Avenue, facing south, circa 1915, the Walter Building housed the Northern Bank of New York's Tremont Branch and a United Cigar store. Upstairs were the offices of the Reliable Insurance Company and of Theodore F. Thompson, architect. Employees of the insurance company can be observed working at their desks through windows thrown open on a bright summer day. The Northern Bank claimed to have a capital surplus of a million dollars and resources of over eight million dollars.

Childhood Summers at Orchard Beach

MARJORIE O'SHAUGHNESSY

Marjorie O'Shaughnessy remembers fondly the early years of the tent-colony summer resort called Orchard Beach, located in Pelham Bay Park on Hunters Island. She evokes in remarkable detail the living conditions, the childhood amusements, the group activities of the temporary residents of Orchard Beach. Mrs. O'Shaughnessy was also fortunate to be an eyewitness to the activities of the naval training camp established nearby during the First World War.

The camp colony at Orchard Beach was a project begun before the First World War by the New York Park Department (not the Parks Department in those days). Occupying the easternmost portion of Pelham Bay Park on Long Island Sound, it was administered and maintained by the department. Originally, it consisted of something over a hundred campsites, close together, on lettered streets. Each street faced a generous lawn, running its length, and unused land stretched beyond in all directions, dotted with rows of fruit trees that gave the place its name. Overgrown fields were bright with clover, goldenrod, and Queen Anne's lace, loud with the cries of crows and bobwhites. In time, more of this vacant land was cleared to make additional campsites available for families who returned year after year. We started spending our summers there when I was three and my sister five.

Although some records of this vanished colony may survive somewhere, we cannot offer a detailed history of it, complete with figures and statistics, only a child's-eye view. Naturally, we ignored mundane consideration of its conception, organization, and management. We accepted it all as though it had been created solely for our benefit. What concerned us most was the crescent-shaped beach at the foot of the hill, the distance of a long city block from our front door. There we scrambled over the rocks dotting the shore and splashed about until the lifeguards took us in hand and taught us to swim properly.

The rocks, appearing immense to small fry, had many uses. We roasted potatoes—mickeys—in their hollows: black and hard on the outside, almost raw on the inside. With sieves and strainers we caught killies in little pools left by receding tides. The fish were placed in a bottle of water and released at the end of each angling session. This pointless occupation was typical of that era. Youngsters were left to devise their own pastimes without the anxious supervision of child-centered parents or the counsel of psychologists. Nor were we given expensive, elaborate play equipment. We had rubber balls, bean bags, bubble pipes, roller skates, jacks, and homemade stilts, kites, and swings. For a group to play mumblety-peg, a single penknife sufficed. Tag and hide-and-seek needed no equipment at all.

Digging for clams at low tide, a very popular diversion even for those like myself who refused to eat a clam, was the essence of simplicity. You threw a rock down on the wet sand. When a thin spout of water rose, indicating a clam's presence below, you dug it up with your hands and tossed it in a pail—for somebody else's dinner, in my case.

When wearied by these various activities, we flung ourselves on the ground to whistle through blades of grass, hunt for four-leaf clovers, blow the tops off puffballs, idly examine the ways of grasshoppers, or study the yellow reflection of a buttercup held under a friend's chin.

Obviously, life was somewhat different and certainly more complicated for the grownups chattering above our heads in the background. They had to be concerned about commuting, coping with oil stoves, oil lamps, and the daily deliveries of food and ice. About these matters we could not have cared less; neither did we share their endless interest in the weather, which was sometimes capable of wreaking havoc against wood and canvas. To us a rainy day merely meant no swimming and no croquet. We stayed indoors to play cards or read the catch-as-catch-can books available: the adventure stories and romances that appear and proliferate in any summer colony. Almost every season saw a certain amount of destruction. When a really wild storm developed, the wind ripped or even blew off the fly—the top layer of canvas—on some of the camps. Sometimes a tree fell, or canoes and rowboats were smashed against the rocks.

After a storm everybody wandered about to inspect the damage. When it was extensive, the owners of the camps affected returned home for a few days until repairs or replacements were made. (We spoke of our homes as being "in the city," of our fathers as working "in the city," although Orchard Beach was, of course, itself a part of the city.)

When the colony was new, the camps must have been fairly primitive, constructed entirely of canvas. As the seasons passed, they sprouted wooden sides halfway up, with metal screening above. Front and back porches were added. Small beds of marigolds, snapdragons, and morning glories were planted, bordered with coleus and bleeding heart, and outlined by clamshells painted white. Flossier types began to refer to their camps as bungalows or cottages and attached rustic signs over the front door spelling out "Rest A While" or "Dew Drop Inn." The final addition was generally a small wooden annex built at the rear to serve as a changing room after swimming.

Simple or elaborate, each camp had to be dismantled at the season's end, leaving only the bare plank floor. Its other components and the furniture were stored through the winter in the small bathhouse at the back. When spring came again, the men of each family, with such relatives and friends as they could entice or bully into helping, retrieved from storage the lumber, canvas, screening, ropes, stakes, tools, and paint, along with the folding chairs and cots. The next several Sundays they spent in reconstructing and refurbishing the camps. No doubt beer and horseplay lightened their labors. Little girls were spared all of this. When we arrived for the summer after school closed, everything was in place, an American flag flapping over each canvas rooftop, the air redolent of fresh paint and newly cut grass.

In the early days, automobiles were comparatively rare. We traveled, I believe, on the New Haven R.R. to Bartow and finished the trip in a horse-drawn hired carriage. Later, a regular bus service from West Farms was instituted and a hack service still later. By then many campers owned cars, which were parked overnight under the apple trees—hand-cranked Reos, Chandlers, Oldsmobiles, Model-T Fords, and occasionally a Velie roadster owned by some dashing bachelor. Having young, unmarried aunts who often spent weekends with us, my sister and I had a large if vague acquaintance with the local blades who whisked them across the City Island Bridge for shore dinners at Thwaites, dancing at the Ben-Hur or the Chateau Laurier, or farther afield to the Pelham Heath Inn or Glen Island. All this seemed much ado about nothing to us, preoccupied as we were with games to play, paper dolls to dress, marshmallows to toast, or feuds to carry on with our own contemporaries.

The outstanding attraction for all the campers was the beach, where everyone congregated at high tide. Swimming had only recently become a popular sport: many adults were still learning to swim. Their attire was a wondrous sight. Men wore dark wool suits with knee-length trunks and short-sleeved tops. The women wore high-laced bathing shoes of cloth and rubber with long black cotton stockings, knee-length dresses usually made of a fabric known as surf satin, over a thin wool undergarment called an Annette Kellerman, after the Australian swimming star of the period. On their heads, covering their abundant hair, they wore fancy turbanlike caps of some waterproof material. Children were bare-legged in short-sleeved, one-piece suits of scratchy wool, which as the season wore on stretched to almost twice their original length.

Wraps were a requisite in going to and from the beach. Perhaps by then specifically designed beach robes had appeared at Deauville and Newport, but at Orchard Beach they were improvised: old bathrobes and kimonos, smocks, overalls and coveralls, well-worn topcoats minus their sleeves and, after World War I, fragments of army uniforms. Everyone recognized everyone else's beachwear on sight. When we arrived to swim, we checked the neat piles of outerwear on the shore to see which of our friends and their families were already in the water.

People went to the beach to swim; sunbathing had not yet become a fad. Tanned skin was not then a status symbol. Being out of doors each day, everyone was tanned by the season's end. One exception to this casual approach was the wife of an actor who later enjoyed many years' run as Papa David in a radio soap opera. She sat under an umbrella, wearing a wide-brimmed hat. As she had very white skin and reddish hair, this may have been a wise precaution, but everyone thought she was affected.

All of living was as informal as the bathing arrangements. Camps were furnished mainly with discards from our winter homes; they were crowded, cozy, and cheerful. The everyday pace was slow, travel rather uncomfortable, walking the usual means of locomotion. The public roads and buildings were lighted by electricity, but there was no electric power in the camps. Pump-drawn water had to be heated on the oil stoves. Our mothers kept house with what they had before the invention of modern household products, labor-saving appliances, or drip-dry fabrics.

There were many advantages to offset these inconveniences. To the average American family, life seemed stable and peaceful. They lived without fear. Crime and violence were unknown in places like Orchard Beach. We had never heard of air or water pollution, drug abuse, or chemicals in foods. Taxes were negligible, unemployment and depression far in the future.

Although life was thus relatively simple, it was not isolated from reality, for the war moved in on us in the summer of 1918, when the U.S. Navy installed a training camp nearby. Suddenly the landscape bristled with young sailors drilling on Shore Road, cheered on by the campers, who rushed out with buckets of cold lemonade and jelly water for their refreshment. Among those trainees were at least two who moved on to postwar fame and fortune: the actor Edward G. Robinson and Thorne Smith, author of the Topper stories.

We children regularly visited the hospital wards, which housed luckless victims of broken bones and noninfectious illnesses, not war wounded. Confined to the premises, they were forced to listen to our singing of "K-K-K-Katy," "Till We Meet Again," and other selections from the wartime hit parade. Young and homesick, they may not have found our efforts really trying, for they were used to homegrown entertainment, a great feature everywhere in those days—and particularly those evenings—before radio and television.

Our elders, like most of that generation, were fond of dancing. A large wooden pavilion located near the camps provided a dance floor and a weathered square piano. A volunteer pianist or a wind-up phonograph generally furnished the music. For occasional Saturday nights, a small dance band, likely to include a saxophone and a banjo, was recruited, and Japanese lanterns added to the gala effect.

On concert evenings, my mother rather wincingly accompanied neighborhood sopranos in Bartlett's "A Dream" and Tosti's "Goodbye." Recitations were offered by little girls who had taken elocution lessons. Following a vanished custom, they learned verses to render with gestures and much expression wherever they found a captive audience.

Amateur theatricals had their devotees: musical revues with a haphazard but willing chorus line in grass skirts and a juvenile in white flannels or plus-fours singing "Whispering" and "Avalon" to ukulele or mandolin accompaniment. And where now are the tenors who leaned against a piano and sang archly about tying apples to the lilac tree? Gone with water wings, fireless cookers, Uncle Sam bars, and gym bloomers!

On other evenings we assembled for outdoor movies—silent, of course. Sitting on the grass at nightfall, we watched Enid Bennett or May McAvoy being pursued by Marc MacDermott and Robert McKim. Because they had dark hair and mustaches, we knew these two were up to no good, although their actual aims eluded us. As film addicts since infancy, however, we knew that the fadeout would find our heroine safe in the arms of Lloyd Hughes, Neil Hamilton, Conrad Nagel, or Richard Dix.

Labor Day climaxed the season at Orchard Beach. Camps were decked with bunting, pennants, and sheaves of goldenrod (nobody had heard of allergies and I don't remember that anyone ever sneezed). Campers of all ages competed in egg-and-spoon races, three-legged races, and other events throughout the day. The final feature was a tug-of-war, with the men divided into teams representing adjacent streets. As the word "dieting" had not entered the American vocabulary either, there were always at least two fathers who weighed close to three hundred pounds. They held the ends of the rope, with slimmer fathers, uncles, and big brothers pulling, yielding, and expostulating in between. As often as not, the tug-of-war went by the board, with both teams collapsing on the ground with laughter.

Except in the memories of graying survivors, nothing but the Sound remains of the Orchard Beach we knew. The last campers left more than forty years ago, when WPA workers began construction of the present large, well-planned public beach to meet the needs of a growing and changing Bronx population.

Memory is notoriously unreliable, hearsay scarcely less so. Common sense tells us that our summers could not have been all laughter, blue skies, and fun, with the Sound forever at high tide; but that is the way we remember them. Each morning was new and shiny, each afternoon we burst forth from our hated naps like released POWs. The smell of new-mown grass under a hot sun, the cool silkiness of salt water against the skin as summer was fading, moonlight reflected on the Sound, falling asleep to the sound of distant dance music, the look of our insteps where barefoot sandals left a pattern in brown and white that lasted past Thanksgiving—all these were ours year after year. And how many children, showered with "advantages," know today the taste and fragrance of real bread, real vanilla in real ice cream, or fruits and vegetables bought from the market gardener's truck the day they were picked?

It is certain that Orchard Beach was a lucky place. In all the years that the campers used oil for cooking and lighting, there was never a fire, which would have caused a wholesale disaster. There was never a drowning in our time, or a serious accident. And the outbreaks of polio, which made parents dread the coming of summer in that period before Salk and Sabin vaccines, never touched Orchard Beach.

Perhaps we children were lucky too, in having been born before parents had ever heard of IQs, peer groups, sibling rivalry, or identity crises. All that was required of us was that we keep healthy, clean, and reasonably quiet at mealtimes. They didn't try to organize our amusements, worry about our interpersonal relationships, or even ask if we were happy. They knew we were.

1975

Entertainment

Metropolis Theatre 142nd St. & 3rd Ave., Bronx, New York City.

LEFT: The Metropolis Theatre, at 142nd Street and Third Avenue, was the first major vaudeville house built in The Bronx. Headlining in the early 1900s is the Cecil Spooner Stock Company which produced plays with Irish themes starring the noted actress Cecil Spooner. A beer garden was located on the theater's roof.

BELOW LEFT: In 1904, Westchester Nicolet Theatre, located on Westchester Avenue, two blocks west of Zerega Avenue, was owned by Adam Hoffmann and managed by George Hoffmann. A new motion picture was shown every day, and admission was a nickel. The Nicolet is reputed to have been the first moving-picture theater in The Bronx.

BELOW: Kane's Casino stood near the end of Soundview Avenue in Clason Point and was a favorite local restaurant. A popular spot for dining, dancing, and special parties and receptions, it boasted that it could seat ten thousand customers. A sign in the roadway in the center of this photograph, circa 1910, directed people to the spot nearby where they could purchase tickets to a ferry that would carry them to the shores of Queens.

A free bath was located off
the coast of Hunt's Point
in the East River circa 1910.
It was designed to be a safe place
for residents of the area to enjoy
the waters.

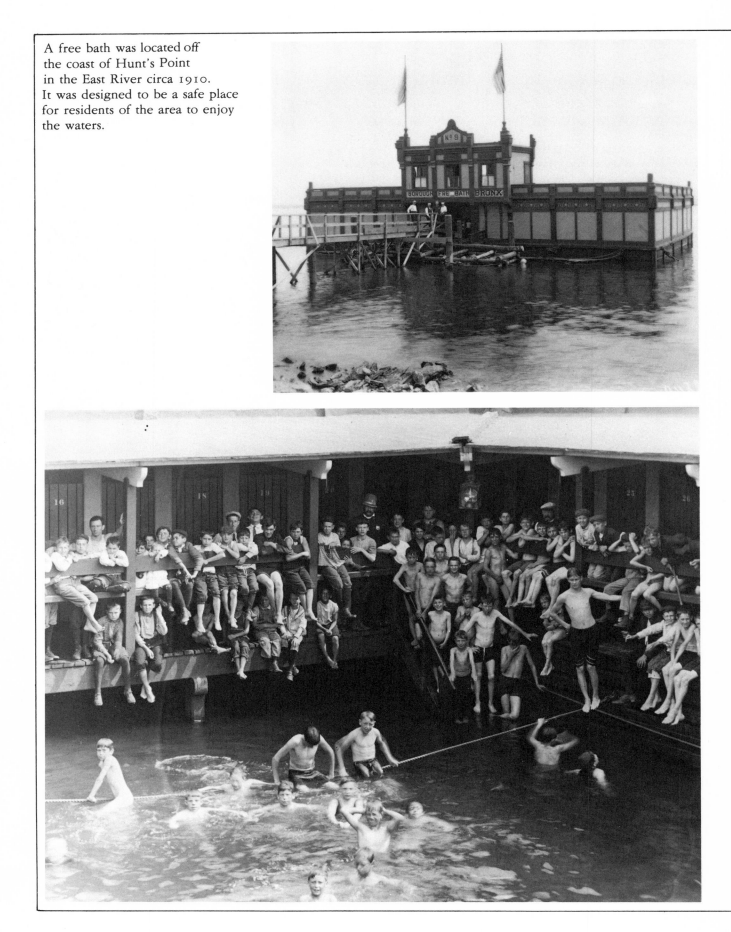

LEFT: Inside the free bath house at Hunt's Point, boys—some fully dressed, some with bathing shorts, and some without any clothes at all —cavort in the water under the watchful eye of a uniformed policeman. The line stretching across the water was a safety rope.

ABOVE: Another free public bath, which was open to both men and women (who entered the building through separate doors), stood on the crest of the 156th Street hill at Elton Avenue in 1914. The city established such public baths as a measure to promote health in areas where apartments did not have their own bathrooms. However, a visit to the baths soon became a social occasion, so much so that many people who had bathrooms in their apartments went to the public facilities as well.

Yankee Stadium is being readied for Opening Day in April 1923. Houses of the sparsely populated area rise behind the bleachers. The Jerome Avenue line of the Lexington Avenue subway, lying between the new stadium and the houses, emerges from its tunnel after passing under Gerard Avenue and curves to pass over River Avenue as an elevated structure, with a station at 161st Street. At the right, Jerome Avenue turns and crosses over the Harlem River into Manhattan via the Macombs Dam Bridge. Commercial and industrial buildings dominate the Bronx riverfront. *(The Daily News)*

West Farms in the Nineties

AGNES P. GARVIN

*Agnes P. Garvin takes us back to her youth in the village of West
Farms in the 1890s. She describes a small, close-knit community
where local people worked in local factories, where travel
was not convenient by modern standards, where malaria was a
danger in summertime, but also where people enjoyed simple
pleasures.*

When my family left Harlem and moved to West Farms in
1891, we found a pleasant little village. The houses on the east
side of Boston Road between 179th and 180th streets date from
this period, as do the homes on the west side of Vyse Avenue
from the Protestant Episcopal church south to Boston Road.

The only means of transportation was the Boston Road car, drawn
by horses, of course. It ran between the village and 129th Street
in Harlem. There were no cars on Tremont Avenue or 180th
Street.

The Third Avenue El ran only to 174th Street at that time. Later,
it was extended to 177th Street and that remained the terminus for
many years.

"Shopping at home" is not so new as folks might think. There
were several very good grocery stores and each owned a horse and
a delivery wagon. On Monday, Wednesday, and Friday, a clerk
called at the home to take an order. The next day the order was
delivered.

The bread and cake man came every day with a basket of bakery
goods. Old Mr. McQuade came round every week and called,
"Pickles! Pickles!" Since most homes were not equipped with gas,
the astral oil man called periodically to keep our lamps filled.
These ranged from a tiny night light to a large and decorative
parlor lamp.

West Farms was well churched. The Roman Catholic church stood
on the northeast corner of Tremont (then Walker) and Bryant
Avenue (then Oostdorp). There were five Protestant
congregations, each meeting in its own building. All children
attended Sunday school and at Christmastime each Sunday school
had a party—no two parties on the same night. Some folks
attended *all* to see which was the best. The children sang songs

and spoke pieces and went home happy with a gift, a box of candy, and an orange.

Public School 65 stood on the site now occupied by P.S. 6. At the end of the eight-year course, pupils who wished to try for college were recommended to take entrance exams for CCNY and Normal (now Hunter) College. The exams at Normal were on eight subjects and occupied the better of three days. In 1896, residents of the area east of the Bronx River became eligible, as did residents of Brooklyn. This raised the number of applicants for Normal to seven hundred plus. P.S. 65 felt proud indeed when one of its applicants attained the highest average in New York City.

Despite its name, West Farms was not a farming community in the nineties. Its residents were mechanics, tradesmen, even factory workers, most of whom walked to work right in the village.

Since the houses were mostly frame structures, there was always work for local carpenters, tinsmiths, plumbers, and painters. When my father was ready to build our home in 1891, he found a little house near Rocking Stone in Bronx Park which was being taken down. The hand-hewn beams, in perfect condition, were bought and went into the new home. That house is still occupied and in excellent condition after seventy years.

Horse-drawn transportation also furnished local employment. Daniel Mapes sold grain, feed, and hay. There were at least three horseshoers as well as a wheelwright, carriage maker, and harness maker.

In addition to food stores, I recall one shoe store and several dressmakers. Nor were the children overlooked. Three candy stores catered to them. There were also a few piano teachers.

The nearest police station was in Tremont and Fire Engine Company 45 occupied its present site, though not the same building, on Tremont Avenue opposite P.S. 6.

One bad feature about the village was the swampy area north and south of Tremont from Daly to Mohegan avenues. It bred mosquitoes and spread malaria. On his first visit to our house, the mailman gave us a slip of paper on which was written "Warburg's Tincture."

"You'd better get a bottle of this at the drugstore," he told us. "It is a quinine preparation and you'll need it unless you are immune to malaria." My father apparently was immune to malaria, but the rest of the family each took a turn at "chills and fever."

75

We had several doctors in the village, including one homeopath. Ever heard of one? Consult your dictionary.

There were two establishments in the village enjoying a goodly number of workers: the Metropolitan Dye Works on the east bank of the Bronx River at 180th Street, and Bolton's Mill on the west bank at Tremont Avenue. The mill was concerned with textiles—among other things, it produced large souvenir handkerchiefs with colored borders.

A relative of mine by marriage, Gavin MacPherson, worked in this mill as a copper roller engraver. He was considered tops in his field and when the mill moved out to Lodi, New Jersey, he was persuaded to move with it. Eventually, however, he returned to live with his son in The Bronx.

South of West Farms Square, parallel to Main Street, now called West Farms Road, flowed the Bronx River. Main Street was the "highway" that ran along the coal and lumber yards that loaded on the river.

The river froze every winter and the ice was cut and stored in the large buildings at Boston Road and what was then called Kingsbridge Road, now Bronx Park South. Later, the Boat House restaurant occupied a site near there, and served good meals and rented rowboats. Great times were had by those who wished to enjoy a trip on the river or a walk along its sylvan shores.

At the first sign of spring, the West Farms folks sought the outdoors. The girls brought out their skipping ropes and their doll carriages and jacks. Jacks seem to be a thing of the past now.

It was a time for taking walks. The "twin parks," Crotona and Bronx, lured many to see the lake that was in one and the river that was in the other. Each of these parks had a bandstand and rows of benches. On Sunday afternoons, these benches were occupied by music lovers who came to hear the concerts—classical as well as popular.

Mothers planned "May parties" for their children, which started out with a parade headed by a king and queen—in proper costume. At the head of the procession was a gay maypole. The Rocking Stone area was a favorite spot, as it was high and dry. Games were played and refreshments were served. A good time was had by all.

1970

76

June Walk Festival

PEARL LONDON BROOKS

Pearl London Brooks concentrates on a moment frozen in time in June of 1921. A single event in St. Mary's Park elicits from her a great deal of information about life in Mott Haven at that time. It also reveals to her the tolerance practiced in a multi-ethnic area.

I wasn't born then, but this is the story that was told to me by my father and mother many years later.

The year was 1921, in June. It was a beautiful sunny day and everyone was getting ready for the June Walk, especially the children. There were handmade costumes and the children were parading around the maypole and in and out of the flower-covered bridges that were also made by hand. The children sang different songs, such as "The May Pole" and "London Bridge." After marching and playing, they would gather together and sit and wait for the cake and ice cream to come.

The best time was when their pictures were taken. The children were so excited; it was not every day that their pictures were taken. In those days, to have a camera was a luxury. The children did not know what a camera was or what it could do. They had an expression of "Look at the birdie" or "Quiet—your picture is being taken." Everyone was afraid to move, although one or two children did because they did not know how fast a picture could be taken. In that year, many people came to live in The Bronx; they came from lower Manhattan, or Brooklyn, or from Europe. There were some farms and few apartment buildings, and many open spaces for people for building. There were horse-drawn trolley cars. And The Bronx had more hills than you can count. The people who came were from different countries and spoke with accents or a broken English (even my father had an accent, which to me was a lovely Russian broken English). My mother was a Polish American. The people were English, Irish, Italian, German, Jewish, Spanish, Greek, Black, Oriental, Russian, and American Indian. They all became friends and learned to get along with one another. Doors were never locked, except at night; in the very hot weather the doors were even kept open. People trusted one another and helped each other, especially when they were in need. This Maypole–June Walk Festival was one way of getting to know everyone and have the children know who lived in the neighborhood and in the surrounding area.

People did not have much money then, or luxuries that they have now. It really was a struggle then, but people were too proud to complain and learned to cope with many situations. They were strong people and not afraid to stand up and do things. They kept their homes and streets clean, although there were plenty of cockroaches and mice around. If the apartment needed plastering, they would learn how to do it, or help each other in their work. In hot weather, children would sleep on fire escapes or on the roof so that they could breathe air. There were no fans then, or air conditioners. Some people who could afford it were able to have a radio, but it was very rare. Children learned to pretend about being something or someone someday. When the movie house was built, it showed silent films and many cartoons. To go to the movies cost only five cents and you could spend the whole day in the movies because you brought lunch. Candy was ten for a cent and all the children would go into the candy shop with a girl or boy who had the penny and share the candy with them. As I look back over the years, I wonder, why can't people get along now? Everyone can have a good life. If only they can learn to have trust in themselves, they will be able to trust each other. Maybe the next generation will be able to do it. I hope so, for if they do, this world will be richer and healthier than it ever was.

Can you picture yourself as a little girl or boy sitting around the maypole, waiting for the ice cream dish to come your way after dancing and singing? There were many other parties, but not like this one, so I was told. But like the saying goes, "We try to better ourselves and so we move away to other places."

1975

People

RIGHT: In the late 1890s, employees of the J. & M. Haffen Brewing Company, located at Melrose Avenue and 152nd Street, strike a formal pose around some kegs of the lager beer they manufacture.

BELOW: American soldiers depart for the Spanish-American War in 1898 from the Van Nest station of the New York, New Haven and Hartford Railroad, at Tremont Avenue and Unionport Road.

ABOVE: Mr. Diehl, the letter carrier for the town of Westchester, stands next to his horse-drawn carriage at the John A. Morris estate in Throggs Neck, in 1909.

BELOW: Members of the Klages family relax at Castle Hill Point in 1914. Ferris Point and Westchester Creek are in the background in the upper left.

The Clason Point Volunteer Life Saving Service, City of New York, was in 1916 one of a whole series of stations along Long Island Sound and the East River staffed by volunteers whose duty it was to save drowning swimmers and disabled boats. Four of the volunteers are wearing Red Cross emblems on their sleeves. Cleats for mooring boats can be seen near the feet of the seated men.

I Remember Old Hunt's Point

EDWARD J. DUFFY

Edward J. Duffy grew up on a dairy farm in Hunt's Point, and tells of the estates and the rambling streets that existed in the village. He also mentions the tragic General Slocum *boating disaster, which eventually led to increased safety regulations on all ships. Perhaps the most valuable of his recollections is the description of Springhurst, a tiny village that completely disappeared in the rapid development of Hunt's Point following the arrival of the subway.*

Hunt's Point at the turn of the century was beautiful. It probably looked the same as it did fifty years before. It consisted of large estates with well-kept mansions and grounds. Some of these homes were still occupied by the original families—the Dickies, Spoffords, Iveses, and a few others. At the end of the old, rambling Hunt's Point Road was the old Hunt mansion built in the early 1700s. This mansion, as I remember it, was partly built of rough stone and lumber. At the east end, there was a tower about forty feet high that resembled a fort. It had windows on several sides which were probably used as lookouts to guard against raids by Indians or by pirates on the Sound. The front of the building had a covered porch the full length of the house. The main entrance led into the living room. The ceilings were low. There was an old open fireplace in the living room that was built with brick brought over from Holland as ballast. A large kitchen was located next to the living room, and there were several other rooms on the first floor. Upstairs were the bedrooms and a large attic with several dormer windows on the east front. On the way down to the house we would pass the old burying ground where the Hunts, the Leggetts, and Joseph Rodman Drake, the famous poet and author of "The American Flag," who had lived in the mansion for a few years, are resting. Across the road was a plot where the slaves once owned by several of the old families were buried.

My father, Hugh Duffy, was a dairyman. He leased a large part of Hunt's Point as a pasture ground for our thirty to thirty-five milk cows. It was my job in the summertime to help the workmen drive the cows to pasture in the morning and watch over them during the day. In the late afternoon, I would drive them back to the barns in the village of Springhurst to be milked.

At the entrance to Hunt's Point Road at Southern Boulevard was a large fenced-in field with ponies and horses roaming around. A large tanbark area, which covered about one square block, was used to house the ponies and horses that belonged to the Simpson estate. It was located on Ives Lane, a short distance from Southern Boulevard and close to the New Haven Railroad line. It had a large circular building with box stalls around the exterior walls. The center part was used to exercise the horses during bad weather. The Simpsons also had a pony ranch down near the end of the point. About 1903, the large tanbark arena was turned into a baseball field, called the Bronx Oval, and many of the big-league stars, such as Heinie Zimmerman of the Chicago Cubs, Tim Jordan of the Brooklyn club, Bugs Raymond of the Giants, Paul Dietz, and Jack Coffey, played there.

The large plant of the American Bank Note Company at Tiffany Street and Lafayette Avenue is located where the old Faile mansion, called "Woodside," once stood. The Faile mansion was built about 1832, and I remember its being demolished about 1908. On the opposite side of Lafayette Avenue stands the Corpus Christi Monastery, which was erected about 1890 and is occupied by the Dominican Sisters.

Many people in the Hunt's Point section today never heard of Springhurst. The village was located on both sides of Longwood Avenue and east of Southern Boulevard. It had a population of about 250 to 300 in the early 1900s. There were two grocery stores and one tavern in the village. Most of the folks used to go to Harlem on the Southern Boulevard trolley to do their shopping. The trolley car took them over the Third Avenue Bridge and around the loop at 129th Street and Third Avenue. There were also several large clothing and department stores on Third Avenue in The Bronx, where the folks did their shopping, and a large butcher store called Webber's, which delivered meat all over The Bronx with two-wheeled carts and fast horses. There was a two-room schoolhouse at Springhurst. The classes there went only to the fourth grade. After that we had to travel by foot to P.S. 25 at Union Avenue and 149th Street. After a year or so, we had to go further to P.S. 27 at St. Ann's Avenue and 148th Street—about a two-mile walk each way. About 1906, P.S. 39 was opened at Kelly Street and Longwood Avenue. That cut down the trip to about six or eight blocks. Some of the children who attended Springhurst School came from Rikers Island and had to row a boat about a mile across the East River and then walk about eight blocks to school. Rikers Island at that time was a city prison as it is today, but on a smaller scale. The children's father was a warden there.

On June 15, 1904, while at Springhurst School, we heard distress whistles from steamboats and fire engines during the morning recess. Looking toward Port Morris and the East River, we saw clouds of smoke coming from a boat on fire. When we went home to lunch, we were told that an excursion boat was on fire. Later that day, we heard that it was the *General Slocum* that had burned, with a loss of over a thousand lives, mostly women and children.

Some of the old lanes in Hunt's Point were still in use in the early 1900s, such as Leggett's Lane, now called Leggett Avenue, and White's Lane, which ran from Southern Boulevard to Westchester Avenue near where Longwood Avenue is today. Ives Lane ran from Southern Boulevard to the Bronx River. It was located just a short distance above Hunt's Point Road. Lafayette Lane ran from Southern Boulevard and Longwood on past Springhurst to Hunt's Point Road. It is now called Lafayette Avenue.

Southern Boulevard was the main thoroughfare at that time, and it was a dirt road up to 1907. By that time, the traffic was getting heavy with the farmers coming down from Hunt's Point, Union Port, Clason Point, and other parts of The Bronx with heavy loads of vegetables. The dirt road made it tough pulling for the horses. Therefore, the city had the road paved with asphalt blocks, which made good riding for trucks, bicycles, and autos, which were just coming along at that time.

About 1904, there were only three houses on Southern Boulevard between 149th Street and Westchester Avenue. There was a small house at Avenue St. John, another one at 156th Street, and an old farmhouse at Hunt's Point Road where the Hunt's Point Palace stands today. From 156th Street to Hunt's Point Road, Southern Boulevard was all vacant land, with brush and woods on the west side and with pasture ground to the east.

Intervale Avenue was a paved road and had no houses from Southern Boulevard to Westchester Avenue, but there was a good-sized brook which ran on the westerly side of the avenue. It originated in Crotona Park and ran under Southern Boulevard to a point about 150 feet south of Longwood Avenue. From that point on, it was called Springhurst Creek. It was also known as Leggett's Creek. Tidewater came in from the East River to the New Haven Railroad tracks and you could row a boat from the East River up to that point. There was good skating there in the winters and crowds came from miles around to enjoy it. During the summer, we went to Duck Island at the end of Tiffany Street to swim, and on weekends, most of the folks in Springhurst went to Barretto Point to bathe and dance. Barretto Point had a small dance hall and bar, a few swings, and a boathouse. On weekends, the music consisted of a piano and a violin. The beach was rocky, and not very good.

I remember my mother's taking the family bathing to Oak Point. At that time, it was the only amusement park in The Bronx. It had a beach, a dance hall, swings, and a carousel. During the summer, small boats made trips from 129th Street and the Harlem River to the Point. Some people came by Southern Boulevard trolley and the New Haven Railroad to the Casanova station, and then walked the long distance to the Point. Oak Point was taken over about 1902 by the New Haven Railroad to be used as a freightyard.

It took us half an hour to walk to Oak Point from where we lived. On the way, we passed close by the Casanova mansion. It was one of the largest mansions in The Bronx, but it had not been occupied for some time. It had been built in 1859 by a grocer named Ben Whitlock for a cost of over $300,000 and was said to have gold knobs on the main entrance doors. The mansion was called Whitlock's Folly. After Whitlock's death, about 1867, his widow sold the house to Señor Casanova, a wealthy Cuban sugar and coffee planter. Casanova was the leader of a band of Cuban patriots, who stored rifles and powder in the dungeons and underground passages of the house. Eventually, the arms found their way to Cuba. About 1890, Casanova moved to New Orleans, and the mansion was left vacant most of the time. It was supposed to be haunted, and we did not get too close until we grew a bit older, when we could get a group together and go through the place from cellar to attic. I remember seeing the brick tunnels running in different directions—one going back to the East River. The Casanova mansion was demolished about 1905, and was replaced by a large piano factory.

During 1905, the Interboro Rapid Transit started running trains through Westchester Avenue, and then up Southern Boulevard to West Farms. This started a building boom, first around the Prospect Avenue station, then around the Simpson Street station, and a few years later, it spread out past Southern Boulevard to Hunt's Point. About 1911, the American Bank Note Company opened its huge plant at Tiffany Street and Lafayette Avenue, where it employed about two thousand people. Whitlock Avenue, now called Bruckner Boulevard, was lined with apartment houses. Hunt's Point was also coming along with one- and two-family homes. Gradually, the old mansions disappeared in the years around 1900–1910.

1965

Transportation

ABOVE: William Habeck drives a carriage on Melrose Avenue and 160th Street in 1890. Mr. Habeck was a cabinet and piano maker. *(Courtesy of The Robert Hall Collection)*

BELOW: At 177th Street and Boston Road in the 1890s, the building on the left shows an advertisement for H. E. Hall, carpenter and builder. A horsecar carries passengers over the muddy roadway. Behind the houses are cultivated lands.

In 1900, the 153rd Street Bridge
over the New York Central
Railroad yards was under
construction to connect Mott
Avenue in the foreground with
Morris Avenue in the distance.
The slope of Cedar Park (later
Franz Sigel Park) can be seen at
the bottom of the photograph. The
large group of brick and frame
houses standing beyond Morris
Avenue is the village of Melrose.

The intersection of 138th Street and Third Avenue, looking north, early in the morning of October 10, 1902, is busy with trolley track construction to handle increased traffic. Trolley No. 449 is going to West Farms. Commercial signs and billboards are plentiful, advertising Gold Dust cleansers, Presto Pastry and Biscuits, Bloomingdale's on 59th Street, a grain feed store, and, on the corner to the right, Rosen's tobacconist at 2550 Third Avenue. Belgian blocks for paving are piled on the east side of the street.

In 1903, the Woodlawn station of the New York Central's Harlem Division, at East 233rd Street, contained the shop of W. Nilsson, florist and landscape designer. It was undoubtedly Nilsson who was responsible for the spectacular floral display beside the tracks, showing a floral clock, the New York City seal, and a complete passenger train. The display commemorated the establishment of the first municipal government in New Amsterdam in 1653. Telephone poles stretch eastward up the hill to White Plains Road.

ABOVE: The area just south of the High Bridge at the edge of the Harlem River was a bustle of railroad activity in 1905. The tracks of the New York Central's Putnam Division (left) and Hudson Division (right) paralleled each other. Raw lumber, extra rails, and cut ties lie amid the sheds between the two sets of tracks. The closer of the two bridges crossing the river to Manhattan is the Putnam Bridge, while the distant one is the Macombs Dam Bridge. The unused piers on the riverbank are in the process of being destroyed. (The sharp lines in the photograph are due to a crack in the glass negative from which this print was made.)

BELOW: Abandoned steamboat piers jut into the Harlem River just south of 167th Street in 1905. The tracks of the New York Central's Putnam and Hudson divisions are at the right. The stone High Bridge arches over the river to bring Croton Reservoir water to Manhattan. Behind it can be seen the lacy steel arches of the Washington Bridge.

No traffic obscures the view looking east on Pelham Avenue (later, Fordham Road) at Webster Avenue in 1908. The steel structures in the middle of the roadway are trusses for a bridge over the tracks of the New York Central's Harlem Division. The railroad station can be seen on the south side of the street, to the right. Crossing above the road are the tracks of the Third Avenue El, whose local station stands at the houselike structure on the platform to the right. The trees to the left mark the grounds of Fordham University.

To the left of the Spuyten Duyvil
station of the New York Central
Railroad in 1908 are the Harlem
River and Inwood Park. To the
right are the Hudson River and, in
the distance, the Palisades.
Passengers had to cross a steel
bridge with wooden planking to
reach the station. Partially
obscured by the sheds in the center
is the swing bridge that connected
the freight rail line to Manhattan.

LEFT: The elevated portion of the Lexington Avenue subway line rises above Westchester Avenue as it crosses Rogers Place in 1909. Dongan Place (later designated as 163rd Street), in the foreground, has been recently repaved. A horse-drawn carriage, seen at the right, is one of the first vehicles to use the new surface. Beyond the elevated structure are two-, three-, and four-story attached dwellings. The backyards are used for hanging wash from clotheslines to dry. Vacant lots are advertised for sale by realtor J. Clarence Davies, whose office was at 149th Street and Third Avenue. The exposed side of the brick apartment house behind the El's pillars to the right of the pole is used to advertise Fletcher's Castoria. The IRT subway cars are about to enter the Intervale Avenue station.

ABOVE: A monorail car rests at the mainland side of the City Island Bridge in Pelham Bay Park, circa 1913. In motion, it rode on the single rail on the ground; while at rest, it was supported by the A-frame which carried the electricity needed to run it.

Growing Up in Morrisania

LEO WEIGERS

Leo Weigers, who is of German descent, grew up in the German enclave of Morrisania. He recalls here the breweries and beer gardens that helped give that village its character, as well as the many activities and amusements available that made growing up there during this period so rewarding.

My family moved from Yorkville to The Bronx in 1906. The area where we lived might be called Morrisania. We first lived on Brook Avenue, in a five-story apartment house between 169th Street and St. Paul's Place. On Webster Avenue, one block west of Brook Avenue, was the thriving moving concern of Julius Kindermann and Son, which remained in business until the late twenties.

Our family attended St. Augustine's Church on East 167th Street between Franklin and Fulton avenues, which stood on an imposing height, and with its twin golden cupolas, standing to this day, and with its vast interior, was called the Cathedral of The Bronx. The pastor was the Reverend Thomas F. Gregg, a very kindly and energetic priest. The parish school had been opened in 1905 with the Sisters of Charity and the Christian Brothers in charge. The Sisters resided in a large frame building next to the school on Franklin Avenue and took in private girl students in what was named St. Augustine's Academy. For several years, the fine Brothers, including the principal, Brother Jerome, traveled to The Bronx daily on the Third Avenue Elevated train from LaSalle Academy on East Second Street and Second Avenue. A restaurant on Third Avenue sent up a hot lunch daily to them at the school. The school registration of boys and girls was approximately 1,200.

One block south on Franklin Avenue stood the immense Second Field Artillery Armory of the New York National Guard. Riding horses could be hired by local equestrians, mostly teachers from P.S. 2 on Third Avenue north of East 169th Street. The armory was famous for its cork-and-tanbark-covered arena where Wild West shows, now called rodeos, would be put on twice every year. Admission was twenty-five cents and featured real live Indians and cowboys. Annually, a food show was also given here, with free admission, and featured all of the Heinz products and a new delicacy—peanut butter. Naturally, it was well attended by the local kids, who gorged themselves on the free samples.

On Third Avenue between East 167th Street and East 169th Street, there were several breweries—Fidelio, Lion, and Liebermann's. Further south, on St. Ann's Avenue and 156th Street, was the famous Eichler brewery. Daily did the pleasant aroma of cooking hops and malt permeate the neighborhood, and one never tired of watching with admiring eyes the splendid white and gray Percheron dray horses pulling the wagons loaded with wooden kegs of good lager beer. Liebermann's also had an abandoned wine cellar known as "the well," where St. Augustine boys settled their differences according to the Marquis of Queensberry rules.

Around 1915, our principal, Brother James, obtained from Colonel Jacob Ruppert the privilege once or twice each spring of being his guest at the Polo Grounds. (Yankee Stadium had not yet been erected.) The seventh and eighth grades filled up two trolley cars chartered by Ruppert to take us to the ballpark and back. Not to be outdone in generosity, "Brother Jimmy" smilingly doled out fifteen cents to each boy from his own pocket to buy hot dogs, Cracker Jacks, or bottled sodas, which then sold for a nickel apiece. As far as I knew, this privilege of free admission to the ballparks originated in our school, and I have never been able to ascertain the contrary.

The area around East 149th Street and Third Avenue was the principal shopping center for all of Morrisania. There was Hearn's, McCrory's (now H. L. Green), and Woolworth's five-and-ten-cent stores on the east side of Third Avenue, and Fennel furniture store on the west side. The Bronx Opera House exhibited the local talent at "Tryout Night," with prizes given to the top three winners and honorable mention in the *Bronx Home News.* The "hook" was used. There was also Miner's-in-The Bronx, which showed two movies and about four vaudeville acts for fifteen to twenty-five cents, and was always crowded. Further uptown at 166th Street and Third Avenue was the local photographer, named Schloss. St. Augustine's school and P.S. 2 on East 170th Street were his principal customers. They were at this location for over thirty-five years. At St. Paul's Place near Third Avenue was a well-patronized entertainment area called Niblo's Garden. It featured a large summer garden with a German band and outdoor dancing, with the usual German cuisine—Hasenpfeffer, pigs' knuckles, and Wiener schnitzel.

At the graduating classes in February and June at St. Augustine's, the principal music was supplied by half the brass marching band (numbering about fifty boys) of the New York Catholic Protectory from the east Bronx. The volume of sound inside a closed and crowded auditorium was simply terrific. The boys wore miniature West Point gray uniforms with knee-length pants and round brass buttons inscribed with NYCP on the jacket front. They also wore black frogs at the cuffs and knees of the pants and the slanted gray garrison caps reminiscent of Civil War soldiers.

The McKinley Square section (169th Street and Boston Road) was an interesting area. There was the McKinley Square Theater, featuring vaudeville acts and movies. As a boy, I saw the first showing of *The Birth of a Nation* there and also the first version of *The Ten Commandments.* These silent films were accompanied by sound effects by the orchestra. The animal acts were boarded at Reilly's livery stables on Clinton Avenue. On Jefferson Place stood Otto Olp's livery stable, where local swains rented out horses and carriages. Cars were few in those days. Mr. Olp also owned a trotting horse, Sir Thomas, that ran on Sundays on the Harlem River Speedway not far from the old Polo Grounds ballpark.

Next door to Reilly's stables stood Hill's garage, which stands to the present day. It ran through from Clinton Avenue to Boston Road. Mr. Hill is said to have become quite wealthy and sold out at the end of World War I and bought a ranch in Arizona. At present, the garage houses a fleet of taxicabs.

John Reilly had a family of five boys and one girl who died in her early teens. He was an undertaker by profession, but hired his own embalmer. He owned two horse-drawn funeral coaches. His funeral parlor was believed to be in the area of East 138th Street and Willis Avenue, as far as we knew. In those days, only the immediate family turned out for funerals. His funeral coaches were heated in cold weather by tin boxes about the size of a brick, each covered with carpeting material. Inside the box was a collection of burning charcoal, and the ladies would rest their feet on it. John, who was affectionately known as "Claypipe Reilly," was notable for one thing: one of his steady pallbearers was a young man, a native of Boston, who later became the redoubtable Walter B. Cooke, who began his mortician's career offering a complete funeral starting at fifty dollars. He was a likable fellow.

Mr. Reilly also had a small trucking business, including three dump trucks with a team of horses to each, and he was in partnership with his brother-in-law, a Johnny McCabe. Their stable and property ran through Clinton Avenue to Boston Road. The boys had a large billy goat for a pet and young Johnny, a son, kept chickens and sold the eggs to neighbors.

In the winter, the Park Department laid off the drivers, and this was the grand opportunity for the kids, including the Reilly sons, to petition Mr. Reilly for the privilege of exercising his horses. We had to fashion our own bridles from the spare harness trunk and then we rode "Reilly's nags" bareback all through and around

Crotona Park. This lasted for three months. Harold, the oldest Reilly boy, was the only one who sported a saddle.

When, in 1916, my family moved to Fordham, I was brokenhearted to leave all this fun behind. As kids we led healthy, normal lives and grew up to be good citizens, a credit to The Bronx and our school and neighborhood.

1972

My Days at Evander Childs

MARGARET GORETH HUNT

Not too many people remember the first years of Evander Childs High School, but Margaret Goreth Hunt certainly does. Through her eyes, we learn about education in The Bronx at the time of the First World War, as well as the concerns and ideas of teenage schoolchildren of that era.

M y family's arrival at the "wilds of The Bronx" from the suburbs of New Jersey in 1914 coincided with the beginning of an era—the start of World War I and the establishment of Evander Childs High School, the second high school in The Bronx.

To begin with, this must have seemed like a far-off dream to the entering students, since there was no building; the upper floors of several elementary schools, and even an old house, scattered all over the upper Bronx, Fordham, Bedford, Wakefield, Unionport, were utilized. The main building, in Westchester, contained the administration, where Gilbert Sykes Blakeley, the principal, held sway. I am sure he was a fine administrator, but his job must have been infinitely easier than such a position is now. I never saw a student disciplined, or need to be, in all my years of high school in The Bronx. Mr. Blakeley, a gentleman of the old school (what other term can I use?), frowned upon football, however, and it was not played by the boys. They played soccer instead, and our beloved Paul B. Mann organized and coached a rifle team, which was always very successful, and kept winning the Whitney Rifle Trophy year after year. As a matter of record, during my senior year, due to the fact that a number of the rifle team had graduated, I was accepted as the only girl. And, I believe, the only girl to win a PSAL letter. We did not, at first, have a rifle range. We used, as did the other schools, a device known as a submachine gun.

Students were accommodated in this fashion until September of 1918, when, at last, students and faculty were gathered under one roof at Creston Avenue and 184th Street. As I never attended, or even saw, any of the annexes, these reminiscences will concern, in the main, only the Westchester building, although I spent my senior year in the completed "new" building.

What a surprise I got on my first day of school. I had just turned thirteen, with my hair down my back (one did not "put up" one's hair until one was sixteen), and I found myself addressed as "Miss

Goreth." The boys were addressed by their last names only. I must say it made me feel a little more grown up!

Although there were trolley lines that ran near many of the buildings, I am sure most of us walked. My friends and I walked about two miles morning and afternoon in all kinds of weather, but I do not remember any very severe snowstorms. It was not only country boys and girls who had a monopoly on walking to school, but, compared to the present development of The Bronx, it was practically country then.

I do not think any school in the country had a more able, well-educated, and dedicated faculty than Evander Childs High School when I was fortunate enough to be there.

There were not too many "frills," except for music, art, physical education (which was increased to five days a week during the war) under Miss Edmunds, and, I think, one course in home economics, or did we call it domestic science? Aside from sports for the boys, the only extracurricular activities were academic clubs: French Club, German Club, etc. One of the English teachers organized the Kit Kat Club, named for a London tavern frequented by Addison and Steele, whose essays were required reading somewhere along the line. We started a story ("Alice Secord Teed Off") and each of us contributed a chapter. There was no plot outline to begin with, so each writer carried along as he wished. Needless to say, it got more lurid as time went on.

The English department was very strong. I remember particularly Dudley H. Miles and Charles Raubicheck. Until Mr. Raubicheck was married, most of the girls had a "crush" on him. I wonder if he knew it?

No time was spent in teaching spelling and grammar; we were supposed to have been thoroughly grounded in those subjects in elementary school. We had plenty of opportunity to put into practice what we had learned, however, by writing compositions and book reports. Reading assignments consisted of at least one of Shakespeare's plays a year, Burke's "Speech on Reconciliation," Carlyle on "Reading," Lamb's *Essays of Elia,* Addison and Steele, a shortened version of Boswell's *Life of Johnson, Idylls of the King,* and, for lighter reading, Stevenson's *Inland Voyage.*

A school magazine was inaugurated—*The Bridge.* The name was chosen as this publication was supposed to bridge the gap among all the annexes. The first editor was BMOC (Big Man on Campus) William Soskin, who somewhat later was half of the publishing house of Soskin and Howells.

History was ably taught by Sophie P. Woodman: ancient history in the sophomore year; medieval and modern history in the junior year; and American history and civics in the senior year.

And imagine three full-time teachers of Latin! Mr. Williams, Mr. A. H. Evans, and Mr. Payne. Even so, there were only six students in my Virgil (fourth-year Latin) class.

Chemistry was taught by Mr. Hannon; and although I elected physics, the name of my instructor escapes me.

Sylvia Coster and Rosabelle MacDonald handled the art department with distinction.

John B. Schamus's elocution classes provided programs for assemblies when there were no outside speakers. I remember William Soskin declaiming a "piece" of which the refrain of each stanza was

> Only the wind and the waves,
> Only the beasts in their caves.

And I rendered a selection about Woodrow Wilson with appropriate gestures:

> "A teacher" [gesture to the right]
> "A student" [gesture to the left]

I am sure that one of our assembly speakers was the renowned Sigmund Spaeth, the Tune Detective. Years later, he was featured on the radio, so he must have been starting his career in 1915.

When we finally got into the new building, Jerry Reynolds organized an orchestra, but it was composed of students who were studying instruments privately. I am sure there was no instruction in school, other than learning to play as a group. We marched to assembly to Schubert's "Marche Militaire" or Sousa's "The Stars and Stripes Forever."

Plays were put on occasionally. My senior class performed *Sherwood,* by Alfred Noyes, in which Catherine Webster, as Shadow of a Leaf, was the outstanding actor.

When we finally found ourselves in one building, there were a great many students to move expeditiously up, down, and around four floors, so a Traffic Squad was instituted to prevent collisions in the halls. I was appointed head of this, which made me eligible for membership in the new chapter of Arista, an honorary society in New York high schools.

Our new building had a library and a swimming pool, which, I think, was never used that first year. I do not know why. There was also a cafeteria, so students, for the first time, could purchase their lunches.

When my children graduated from a central high school in upstate New York, I found for the first time that there was such a thing as a Regents Diploma in addition to the diploma from the school itself. Perhaps the reason for not granting such a certificate in New York schools was that the standards of New York City high schools were so much higher than those required for a Regents Diploma that the Regents Diploma would be supererogatory (as the president of Bryn Mawr is said to have replied when questioned about the absence of a chapter of Phi Beta Kappa there).

Biology, a required freshman course, was rather elementary compared to the course now, and it and zoology were taught by Paul B. Mann.

The mathematics department was headed by Henry I. Norr, who later succeeded Gilbert S. Blakeley as principal. For the academic (college preparatory) course, elementary algebra, plane geometry, and intermediate algebra were required, after which I, personally, was glad to call it quits.

I really should not fail to mention the clothes we wore. Middy blouses were almost standard for girls, and even the best-dressed girls in school had very few changes. We were neither the fashion plates of the fifties nor the slovenly objects of today. The boys wore knickers and long black stockings. And about this time, low-cut "oxfords" came in, replacing high shoes that both boys and girls had worn. Buttonhooks became obsolete!

As for foreign languages, up to World War I, both French and German were offered in addition to Latin. When the United States entered the war, German was dropped, and I believe Spanish may have taken its place. Miss Heuermann and Mr. Schoenberg taught German and Paul Eldredge handled the French. Many years later, I read a short story of his in a national magazine, but I do not know how much of a career he made with his writing.

I see I have said nothing about sports for girls. That is because there were none. We played a little basketball, but the facilities in the early days were pretty meager. One fall, there was an attempt to organize a field hockey team, but this entailed a trolley ride to Van Cortlandt Park after school and, without Daylight Saving Time, there was not much daylight left later in the fall. It petered out.

My last recollection, except for my graduation, was Armistice Day. Mr. Blakeley assembled the whole school on the front step. After announcing the cessation of hostilities, his next words were "I have no authority to dismiss you . . . ." The rest of his words went unheard. The crowd of students, most of whom had never cut a class in their lives, just melted away—all but a few "greasy grinds" who went back into the school, so we heard the next day. A friend of mine and I had the foresight to take the subway and go downtown and walk the length of Fifth Avenue, where we saw the impromptu celebration at the end of "the war to end all wars!"

One other memory I have is of leading Evander Childs High School in the Bronx Borough Day parade. I wore a white skirt, white middy blouse, and a white sailor hat.

I have pointed out how superior the faculty of Evander Childs was, but I must mention that the student body was composed of very talented and unusual people too. They were "nice kids" and really concerned about getting an education. The girls did not feel discriminated against; we respected the faculty and they respected us, and really tried to help us. We did not need a PTA. We tacitly acknowledged, but did not feel oppressed by, the "generation gap," and I think we went out from Evander to college, to business (Yes, Virginia: girls even then did expect to earn their own living—at least until they got married), or to homemaking, as well prepared as or, in some ways, better prepared than students of today.

1980

Schools

The Catholic Protectory, on Unionport Road (seen here looking toward Tremont Avenue), was run by the Catholic Church as an institution for orphans and wayward children. The children lived, were schooled, and were taught a trade here. Discipline was highly regarded, and frequently judges would sentence delinquent boys to live in the protectory in order to salvage their lives. The playground and field were used by the public as well as by semiprofessional ball players. The protectory was near the Morris Park racetrack, which can be seen at the upper right in this 1899 photo. Between the track and the protectory is the New York, New Haven and Hartford Railroad.

The Catholic Protectory Band,
seen here at an 1899 band contest,
stands in front of the Clason
Military Academy, off Soundview
Avenue in Clason Point. This band
was the most famous in The Bronx
at the time.

ABOVE: In the bakery of the Catholic Protectory in 1899, the man with the mustache is obviously the master baker, and the boys his apprentices. The bread was taken from the oven in huge slabs and then broken into loaves. The staff apparently used Snowball Choice flour.

LEFT: A cooking classroom in the Catholic Protectory girls' division, circa 1900, contains anatomy drawings of animals on its walls and teapots on its tables. All the necessary cooking apparatus is neatly stored in wooden cabinets.

Public School No. 12, WESTCHESTER, N. Y. City.

RIGHT: P.S. 12, located near Westchester Square, was the major public school in the eastern part of The Bronx in 1910.

BELOW: Morris High School, the American flag flying atop its Gothic tower, dominates the impressive homes in front of it near 166th Street and Boston Road, circa 1910. The town houses to the right, facing Trinity Avenue, have small backyards which contain clotheslines.

Aquinas Hall, operated by the
Sparkhill Dominican Sisters as a
school for young girls, was housed
in the old Grote Mansion. In this
1923 view, East 182nd Street
crosses in front of the school,
while the Notre Dame Home for
the Aged rises to its rear. The
brick building across Belmont
Avenue, to the left of the school,
is the Belmont firehouse.

The Story of My Boyhood Days in Highbridge

CHARLES J. CASAZZA

Charles J. Casazza tells of his youth in Highbridge and University Heights. Both villages had a rural atmosphere, with farms within easy walking distance. Mr. Casazza lived on a farm in University Heights while attending a school that abutted another farm.

I was born on May 1, 1892, at 67 President Street, Brooklyn. I did not know much about Brooklyn, because when I moved to my new home in the beautiful Bronx, I was six years old. My dear father, who always gave me and my family a nice home to live in, purchased a frame house at 169th Street and Inwood Avenue, which was one of the many beautiful places in The Bronx. My home was really in a valley, for which The Bronx was known in many places.

I can remember the Ruhlion pickle factory, where we boys were welcome anytime to as many pickles as we cared to eat. I loved the sweet ones.

My first school was nearby, and to this day still stands. It is still known as P.S. 11, near Boscobel and University avenues in the Highbridge section of The Bronx.

The neighborhood derived its name from the High Bridge, which spanned the Harlem River. The bridge was a water carrier to Manhattan. This was, up to 1895, the only way that Manhattan got its water supply. No vehicular traffic could pass over this bridge and no road approach to this bridge was in evidence. The bridge itself had a set of pipes in which the water flowed.

On University Avenue, on many occasions, one could find cows browsing nearby. At this time, University Avenue was a dirt road, twenty-one feet wide at most, and was called Aqueduct Avenue. On each side was plenty of fine green grass. On the east side of this avenue to Jerome Avenue were farms going from Burnside Avenue north to 181st Street.

Jerome Avenue in those years was a redbrick road with a trolley line that ran from 155th Street north to Yonkers Avenue. Jerome Avenue above 233rd Street also was known as Central Avenue. We, especially on a warm Sunday, would take this trolley ride in opened trolley cars from the start of the line to the end for a nickel. As a matter of fact, one could ride the whole Bronx for this price by use of a transfer with several tear-off tabs. This would allow one to ride on any intersecting line after paying a nickel just once.

What I really was very fond of was the west side of University Avenue in the springtime. From 181st Street to Featherbed Lane was an enclosed Sisters' Home, which had a wall about four feet high. Along the top of the wall were lilac bushes, which were just full of lovely blossoms, and the smell ranged as far as the end of this wall.

After living at 169th Street and Inwood Avenue for a number of years, my dear father decided to move further north. He bought an attached house at 67 West 183rd Street. Here, I really enjoyed the rest of my boyhood days. Behind my home was a beautiful farm with cows, horses, chickens, and whatever. It was called Collins' Farm. Many times, with the permission of Mr. Collins, I, with my boyfriends, would gather apples (red and green varieties), pears (Seckel or Bartlett), or whatever was ripe at the time.

My next school of attendance was P.S. 26, which still stands. Behind our school was also a beautiful farm owned by New York University. We could reach out of our classroom window and pluck nice, juicy apples, providing the teacher did not catch us.

Across from our school was a large oval formerly used for bicycle races. There, we would hold our athletic events against other schools. I won a silver medal for the hundred-yard dash. I came in second; if I had come in first, I would have won the gold one. In later years, when I became a young man, this oval was taken over by a builder who built apartment houses there and named them the Berkley Apartments, which can be seen today. The oval had been known as Berkley Oval.

Across University Avenue on the east side of our school was the Holy Spirit Church, where I received my first Holy Communion and Confirmation. I still have the white ribbon for Communion, and the red one for Confirmation, given to every child by Cardinal Hayes, who administered this beautiful event, along with a Holy Name book, which I still also have. I am very proud that Cardinal Hayes performed these holy deeds. When I became a man, I am proud to say I was chosen by the Knights of Columbus to stand with three other Knights as honor guard at his wake at St. Patrick's Cathedral. I shall never forget this as long as I live, for he was loved by young and old.

When I was a boy, I used to enjoy a walk through the daisies, violets, and black-eyed Susans on the aqueduct, which was the water tunnel that supplied water to the High Bridge from Croton Dam, many miles north of The Bronx. This aqueduct, especially at the spring of the year, was beautiful. We boys picked many bunches of the various blossoms and sold them to the many rich people who came there for their vacation.

The rich used horse-drawn carriages for conveyance, and would never fail to stop at the Charles Inn, which was located north of Gun Hill Road at the corner of 213th Street. We boys always enjoyed the Tally-ho, which was drawn by six brown horses and driven by two men who were dressed in red uniforms. It also carried a footman. These footmen would sound their trumpets when they would arrive at Gun Hill Road, or just before they would arrive at the inn. There, they would freshen up and have lunch. We boys used to go there quite often to see our great fighters train for their next bout. There were fighters like Jack Johnson, Stanley Ketchel, and many other great athletes.

I thank God for giving me a very happy life with many memories.

1978

Oh, Memories

CLAUDE HYMAN

*Claude Hyman's memories of Throggs Neck and Sound View are
particularly valuable because of the relative paucity of descriptions
of these areas in the innocent years. Fewer people lived in these
rural areas than in other parts of The Bronx, and, thus, fewer
accounts have survived. Throggs Neck and Sound View were so
sparsely populated that they retained their rural atmosphere even
after the First World War.*

I was originally attracted to the Valentine-Varian House when I
saw the statue of the Civil War soldier standing on the lawn. The
statue of the old Bronx River soldier brought back memories of
my boyhood.

When I was in my teens, and even earlier, I would walk past that
statue and see him maintain his lonely vigil in the middle of the
Bronx River at Gun Hill Road. I noticed later that the statue had
disappeared, and was pleasantly surprised to see it standing guard
in front of the Valentine-Varian House. It is in excellent hands
now and may it remain there forever.

Not long after World War I, I delivered mail out of the
Westchester Square post office to the residents of East Tremont
Avenue in The Bronx, near Fort Schuyler. There's nothing unusual
about that, but what is unusual is that I delivered this mail with a
hired horse and buggy! East Tremont Avenue at that time, I
remember, was a two-lane country road with no bus or trolley
service. The countryside was reminiscent of present rural upstate
New York. I recall sitting on a stone fence and eating my lunch
while the horse ate his and then grazed on the grass. The horse
knew the route and I would simply let him go from mailbox to
mailbox by himself. The mailboxes were on the side of the road
just like the present RFD mailboxes.

I recently took a bus ride through East Tremont Avenue. Gone
were the two-lane roads, the stone fence, the open fields, the
farms, and the horses. In its place were broad streets, private
homes, stores, and the East Tremont Avenue bus. But I still fondly
remember East Tremont Avenue as a pretty two-lane country road.

Sound View Avenue at that period had farms. The farm owners
owned goats. These goats were milked by their owners. No
containers of milk at forty-three cents a container! I also remember

that police patrolled regularly on bicycles up and down Sound View Avenue.

When I was nine years old, I would occasionally walk past the 52nd Precinct station house on Webster Avenue and Mosholu Parkway. About four years ago, I moved back into my boyhood neighborhood and I again walked past the 52nd Precinct station house. To my amazement, it was exactly as I remember seeing it as a nine-year-old boy. Not a stone was changed!

Oh, memories! The amazing thing is that I have enjoyed visiting national shrines like Valley Forge and Gettysburg, but we have a little-appreciated shrine right here on Bainbridge Avenue: the Valentine-Varian House, the Museum of Bronx History.

1978

Colleges and Universities

In 1904, a viewer looking north on New York University's uptown campus would see a monument on the mound to the left of the tennis courts. It is actually a remnant of the original NYU building at Washington Square. Behind the monument and across Hall of Fame Terrace is the residence of the University's Chancellor, Henry Mitchell MacCracken.

ABOVE: In 1910, Fordham University's parade ground was a center of college activities. Dealy Hall, at the left, served as a residence and classroom building. The Administration Building stands at the center, while Hughes Hall, to the right, housed Fordham Prep. The parade ground itself was used for college sports and parades of the college's corps of cadets. *(Courtesy of Fordham University Archives)*

BELOW: Manhattan College Quadrangle was under construction in 1923. Located on Spuyten Duyvil Parkway, the site was to be the new home of the college after it moved from 131st Street and Broadway in Manhattan. *(Courtesy of the Manhattan College Archives)*

In a 1920 aerial view of New
York University's uptown campus,
the curved road marks Hall of
Fame Terrace, which connects
University Avenue, at the bottom,
with Sedgwick Avenue, at the top.
The football field at the center of
the photograph is Ohio Field.
Above and to the right of the
football field are tennis courts. The
rotunda of the Gould Memorial
Library is flanked by Language
Hall and Philosophy Hall, with the
Hall of Fame standing behind.

My Childhood Days in Williamsbridge

HELEN A. ROSE

Helen A. Rose writes about the village of Williamsbridge in the north central section of The Bronx before 1925. Far from the center of the growing city, and among the last places to receive the benefits of subway service, Williamsbridge retained its village character longer than most other areas of The Bronx. Mrs. Rose describes this character in accurate detail, as well as discerning the beginning of the changes that would alter the area.

I remember, not the "house where I was born" (since my family moved to Williamsbridge when I was three months old), but the one in which I grew up. It was a three-story frame house with a large yard and an iron fence. Since the other houses on the block had picket fences, ours was always known as "the house with the iron fence." The house and the fence are still there on 214th Street between Bronxwood and Paulding Avenues.

Memory, at times, being a tricky affair, I am not sure of the chronological order of some events (they occurred more than fifty years ago), but I put them down as they come to my mind.

One street was a dirt road that yearly was tarred to keep down the dust. The sidewalks in the whole neighborhood were, for the most part, covered with cinders, though a few were of flagstone. These, along with 217th Street, which, for some unknown reason, had a cement walk from White Plains Road to Paulding Avenue, were the places used for roller skating.

Going to school meant walking in all kinds of weather to P.S. 41 at Olinville Avenue and Magenta Street, passing by the firehouse, where horses were used to pull the engines, and the post office, now moved to Gun Hill Road.

The southeast corner of Gun Hill Road and White Plains Road was a rocky cliff, probably ten to fifteen feet high, and it was the custom to stand on top of it to watch the fireworks display each July 4th, after which we took a quart milk pail and went to Rippey's candy store for ice cream, hurrying home as fast as possible so it would not all be melted by the time we got there.

White Plains Road looked very different then. Below Gun Hill Road, there was the Pizzatello stoneworks and, south of that, a few houses and stores. The Allerton Avenue section was large fields where we picked daisies in huge bunches to be used to decorate the church sanctuary for Children's Day, an occasion when little girls in white dresses with gaily colored sashes and hair ribbons, hair "crimped" with an iron heated on the stove, or put up in rags, or "kid curlers," the night before, and boys in knickers and white shirts, "said pieces" appropriate to the occasion.

Gun Hill Road also meant von de Hyde grain and feed store, the statue of the Bronx River Soldier, and the Immaculate Conception Church, a small frame building on the northeast corner of Holland Avenue. On certain feast days, an outdoor festival was held and booths, lighted by some sort of gas lamps, sold exotic goods, as they were dishes relished by our Italian neighbors, who made up the larger part of the congregation. Other Catholic parishioners attended St. Mary's Church, which was, and still is, at 215th Street and White Plains Road, although it now is considerably changed in appearance.

At 214th Street and White Plains Road, Schleuter's had a grocery and made deliveries to the house (after coming for the order) by horse and wagon. Nearby was Kostrin's dry goods store. "Benny" seemed to be the favorite salesman. A harness shop was just north of Rabin's, the paint store which stood next to Kostrin's. Boeder's drugstore, a landmark in the neighborhood because of the large mortar and pestle on the roof of the building, was at 215th Street. I well remember the bottles of colored water in the windows, which signified the type of business. (Barber poles were in front of the barbershops, and could be spotted from quite a distance.)

It was many years ago that the building at 216th Street and Willett Avenue, across from the old (and still in use) P.S. 13, was a YMCA. Now it houses the Moose Hall.

Emmanuel Baptist Church, which was originally located in a small frame building on 220th Street just west of White Plains Road, occupied (and still does) a large plot of land north of 216th Street, and was known either as "the red church," because of being built of red brick, or "the Church on the Hill," as it is some twenty or more steps above the sidewalk level.

Three doctors were "next-door neighbors" at 217th Street—Dr. Shirmer, Dr. Gillespie, and Dr. Oaks. Later, each moved to a different location. Dr. Pinckney's house and office was on a rise of ground on the northeast corner of 213th Street and White Plains Road, and just behind it was his carriage house. He had the distinction of having a colored man who took care of his horse and was his driver when he made his house calls (which all doctors did then!).

Old Crawford Memorial M.E. Church, named for the Crawford family, was at 218th Street, and was often referred to as "the green church," as it was built of a green limestone, or sometimes as "the 'God Is Love' Church," as it had that inscription over the front door. All the community was upset when it was destroyed by fire in the 1920s. A benefit for the building fund for the new church was held in the "new" B.B. Theater at 224th Street—a production of *Pinafore* put on by the members of the church. Services, until the new building was ready, were held in the Masonic Temple on 216th Street. For many years, the organist at Crawford was Wilbur Varian, who had married "one of the Crawford girls."

Johnson's butcher shop was near 219th Street and Mr. Johnson and his helpers were usually garbed in long white aprons and wore stiff straw hats.

Bauer's bakery was on the northwest corner of 220th Street and it was a big occasion when the B.B. Theater was opened just up the street from them. Before that, "going to the movies" meant going to the outdoor place at 228th Street and White Plains Road, the Nickelette, just below Goblin's bakery on 216th Street (now the site of an Italian pastry shop). When that closed, there was the movie house on 217th Street, just east of White Plains Road. There, there would be an intermission, during which the ushers went up and down the aisles selling lollipops and Tootsie Rolls, or sometimes Necco Wafers. For several years, there was an outdoor movie on 222nd Street and White Plains Road on the northwest corner.

In those days, all the Protestant churches held evening services on Sunday, and it was the custom of a group (which included my family) to go down after the service into the basement of either Bauer's or Goblin's, where the baking was done, and buy buns fresh from the oven and then stand on the corner (in good weather), or go into Ramm's ice cream parlor on 219th Street, order a hot chocolate, and eat the buns. How well I recall the delicious smell of the bread being taken on a peel from the ovens built into the basement walls! Sometimes we could buy a loaf of bread or some rolls to take home. Buns or rolls in those "dear, dead days" were six for five cents, and the bread, ten cents a loaf.

East of Goblin's was the stable where Ballard, the undertaker, kept his horses and carriages, and next to that, the blacksmith's shop. Just as in Longfellow's poem "The Village Blacksmith," the "children coming home from school/Look[ed] in at the open door." Ballard's funeral parlor, with living quarters above it, was the only building on White Plains Road between 216th and 217th Streets.

James Butler's grocery occupied the northeast corner of 217th Street and next to it was Spokony's dry goods store, which was a rival of Kostrin's. Rippey's ice cream parlor was in the next store, and on the 218th Street corner stood the Bronx Borough Bank, a fairly imposing structure in those days.

The police station was, and still is (although it will soon be replaced by a new building further east), at the northwest corner of 229th Street, and the "upper firehouse" was next to it. It was an interesting and exciting sight to see the engines pulled by the fine pairs of horses dashing up or down the avenue. When the engines became mechanized, and had trouble going on the icy roads, the people standing on the sidewalks would call out, "Go back to the horses."

Two Hundred Twenty-second Street, from Carpenter Avenue to White Plains Road (and further east), being an extra wide street, was for several years used for a street carnival. This brought large crowds to go to the rides and play the various games.

The first library in Williamsbridge was in a very small store on the south side of 219th Street, just west of White Plains Road. Later, it moved to a larger room behind the Weiss saloon at 223rd Street. Still later, it moved to its own fine building in back of the police station at 229th Street.

Traveling in those days was quite a bit different from now. When you went downtown, it meant taking the trolley on White Plains Road to either West Farms to get the subway, or to the Bronx Park terminal of the Third Avenue El, just opposite 198th Street. The station was approached by a high stairway and a long covered bridge over the New York Central Railroad tracks. Well I remember on cold winter nights coming home from Manhattan, standing in a doorway at either station, waiting for the trolley. Of course, in summer, it was fun riding on the open cars, both trolley and El. Trolleys also went north, and by means of transfers from line to line, we could go to Glen Island, where there was not only a beach but also a fine picnic grove and an amusement park. This was most often the scene of our Sunday school picnics. A longer ride would land us at Hudson Park, where we could get a boat, or in New Rochelle, where we got a trolley to Rye Beach. That was a trip!

Beyond Paulding Avenue from Gun Hill Road north was mainly woods. The Stickney estate (now the site of the Lavelle School) was one of the larger pieces of property. Boston Road was, for many years, a dirt road. Zahn's pig farm was located on it below Gun Hill Road, and I recall the night it burned. Squealing pigs ran in every direction.

Mr. Reinheimer was our milkman. He had a small herd of cows in the barn behind his house on Tilden Street, where there is now a high-rise apartment. At times in the spring, when the cows were taken out to pasture over toward Boston Road, and they dined on wild onions, the milk would have a very peculiar taste.

Located on the northeast corner of 222nd Street and White Plains Road stood the Havens house. In the side yard was a small cannon, and rumor had it that "Washington slept here on his way to or from White Plains." I've never known the truth of this statement. In about the 1930s, the house went out of the family, was bought and moved to 222nd Street near Barnes Avenue, turned so that what was the side became the front, and it has been so completely changed that no one would ever recognize it.

There are other fragments of images that enter my memory: watching a dead horse being removed from the street; the ice wagon that came each day, and "Tony," who gave the children chips of ice; the "waffle man," who came in a horse-drawn wagon, very occasionally, but who brought great excitement to the children; the excitement and wonder when the Whittle family house was moved from 220th Street near White Plains Road to "our" street.

Another vivid memory is looking out of our attic window and seeing the first subway train pulling into the Gun Hill Road station. It was a shuttle and it arrived from East 180th Street, where the trains to and from downtown terminated. When the El first came up above Bedford Park, it too was a shuttle, coming to 219th Street and returning to Fordham Road, where one got the City Hall trains.

1971

Landmarks

St. Raymond's Church with its
wooden bell tower (seen in 1897)
was located at Tremont and Castle
Hill avenues. The churchyard of
this oldest Catholic parish in The
Bronx is in the foreground of the
photograph.

ABOVE: The Gouverneur Morris mansion still stood at the southern end of The Bronx near Cypress Avenue, circa 1900. In 1906, the New York, New Haven and Hartford Railroad tore it down, over the protest of several local residents, to make way for a railroad yard.

BELOW: A photograph taken on Decoration Day, circa 1900, shows West Farms Soldiers' Cemetery, at 180th Street and Bryant Avenue, the final resting place of many soldiers of the Civil War. A statue of a Union soldier guarded the graves. The Beck Memorial Presbyterian Church is on the right.

The Valentine-Varian House, which witnessed numerous battles during the American Revolution, was located on Van Cortlandt Avenue East before Woodlawn Road (now Bainbridge Avenue) was built. In 1900, the fieldstone farmhouse stood on a dirt road which was once part of the original Boston Post Road but which had become merely a lane that connected the villages of Williamsbridge and Kingsbridge.

ABOVE: The Van Cortlandt house, in Van Cortlandt Park, had recently been converted from a Park Department building to a museum chronicling its colonial and Revolutionary War heritage when this photograph was taken, circa 1900. The statue of General Porter at the right of the house memorializes the man who revived the New York State National Guard. The statue faces the parade ground where his troops often drilled.

BELOW: In 1901, the Edgar Allan Poe Cottage still occupied its original site on Kingsbridge Road. It was owned by a dentist named Chauvet, a French immigrant who rented it to a tenant. A hitching post stands in front of the gate to the right and a streetlamp and fire hydrant stand on the sidewalk in the center. Kingsbridge Road has a dirt roadway.

The Hearn Mausoleum in
Woodlawn Cemetery was under
construction by the Thompson
Brothers in 1903. Hearn was the
owner of Hearn's department
store. The two men in uniform are
cemetery guards.

LEFT: The grounds of the vast Wave Hill estate of financier George W. Perkins, at Independence Avenue and 252nd Street, seen here in 1911, overlooked the majestic Hudson River and the New Jersey Palisades. The lawn ending at the balustrade nearest the river also served as the roof of an underground recreation area, which included a bowling alley and a squash court. A pergola at the left crowns another balustrade overlooking the lawn. *(Courtesy of Wave Hill)*

ABOVE: Parson's Windmill, seen here in 1912, stood on the east bank of Westchester Creek just north of today's Bruckner Expressway traffic circle. It serviced a plant nursery and greenhouse. In 1890, the windmill was noted on mariners' charts.

My Mott Haven

MARY W. KELLER

Mary W. Keller recalls here a Mott Haven of villas, small apartment houses, and open spaces, and discusses her experiences in the Immaculate Conception School in nearby Melrose. She, too, was a witness to the beginnings of change caused by the building of the subway and the advent of the automobile.

I was born on July 4, 1894, in Chicago, Illinois, and, in 1901, when I was seven years old, Father was transferred to New York.

For the first six months, we lived on the second floor of an old brownstone house on West 98th Street and Amsterdam Avenue. Then, an old friend of Father told him about the advantages of The Bronx. Father investigated and promptly found a very lovely four-room apartment with bath, steam heat, and hot water. The building had the prettiest vestibule and lovely carpeted halls which the janitor kept up. All of this was for seventeen dollars a month.

There was a "catch" connected with the low rent. The subway was being built under 149th Street between the river and Third Avenue, and our apartment was at the corner of 149th Street and Walton Avenue.

Every few days, all the tenants were summoned to the basement for safety while the workmen blasted. During the two years it took to complete the subway, we children became very friendly with the workers, and the day the first train went from Mott Avenue to Third Avenue and 149th (July 10, 1905), the foreman gave us very young children (about six of us) flags to carry, and we were passengers on the first trip in the first coach. Never in my life have I forgotten that ride.

From the two windows in our living room, we looked out at a very beautiful estate occupied by the Stephens Coal Company owners. It was a lovely old house, a lot of acres and a big hill. At the bottom of the hill was a huge, luxuriant oak tree. Mr. Stephens came over to the janitor of our building and said to use the grounds. In winter, the snowy hill gave us many long rides, and in summer, the beautiful tree served us for picnics, and May parties complete with a maypole. When the weather was warm, our mothers would come with us. Every morning, the groom would bring the horse around for the Stephens daughters to ride. What a delightful place to call home, and how we enjoyed our childhood days! I had two little sisters. One was born there.

Every morning at seven-thirty, my sister Elizabeth and I started to walk to Immaculate Conception School, located at 150th Street and Melrose Avenue. We had to be there at seven fifty-five for eight o'clock Mass. It certainly was a fine, outstanding school, operated by the Sisters of Christian Charity, and I went there for eight years. We were taught religion, the "three Rs," English literature, elocution, singing, and typing. All of us could read extremely well. I recall we had algebra in the fifth grade. When I left, I could speak, read and write German, type, and sew. Every Friday afternoon, we had sewing and story-reading time. There were about thirty-two pupils, and the class was in two sections, A and B. The A section were quick learners, and more time was given to the B section, as learning was not so easy for them.

For all the years, I sat next to a darling person, Eugenia Kalbacher, now in Florida, and we have been friends since 1902. We call each other every other week and correspond. We have never lost track of each other in seventy-seven years. All of the pupils were German, of fairly affluent families, and we were easy to manage. I was the only non-German: Mary MacMullen.

The boys played a game they called Kick the Can, and all of the girls had dear little German bisque dolls about six inches high with real hair and eyes that opened and shut; they sold for twenty-five cents, and we were quite content making doll clothes. There was roller skating too, and we enjoyed playing tag.

Sometimes, on Sunday, the family walked to the Polo Grounds to see the ball games, and often we went to band concerts in Franz Sigel Park.

There was a free boathouse at 155th Street and the river, and we walked by many nice empty houses on Gerard Avenue to get there. It was well supervised, and we had a lifeguard who taught us to swim and dive. The matron was sweet and kind to us.

I recall that at 149th Street and Gerard in the vacant lot was a huge stone which they claimed was a meteorite. It always fascinated me.

As I remember, the children were all well behaved. We really loved each other.

We had a dedicated doctor on Mott Avenue and 150th Street. Dr. Pringle was a kind, handsome man. He made house calls for one dollar, and was always available.

In 1904, we saw the first auto come over the bridge, and we were terrified at the speed—ten miles an hour.

The houses between 138th and 152nd streets on Walton Avenue were very large and stately. The families all had servants and gardeners. From Mott Avenue to Walton Avenue and 149th Street, there was a row of yellow brick town houses, well kept. Besides our building, there was an old redbrick apartment building covered on many walls with ivy vines. We all knew each other and were great friends.

Before we could boast of using an old "icebox," we used the fire escape window in winter weather, and in hot weather we bought our food every day at a grocer and butcher close by our home. Being the oldest, I learned very young how to shop.

By the way, our bathtub was of tin and wood.

On opposite corners at Third Avenue and 150th Street were two lovely department stores, Brill's and Rogers'. Ribbed hosiery sold for fifteen cents, good girdles for twenty-five cents, and fine leather purses for twenty-five cents.

Mother made us elegant cloaks for many years, and yard goods were fifteen cents, and wool was forty-nine cents. We all wore two petticoats, one flannel, and one cotton, trimmed with elaborate embroidery. We wore pretty aprons, and the nuns made us leave them on hooks in the schoolroom to keep them clean much longer.

Next to Brill's was an old-fashioned ice cream parlor, and ice cream sodas (big ones, too) were five cents each. The mahogany woodwork in the shop was handsome, and so were the huge mirrors. We were usually given five cents on Sunday for ice cream. There were no charge accounts and credit cards in The Bronx, and to owe money was a huge disgrace and worry. Today, if you do not owe money, you are considered a "poor risk."

We were all heartbroken when we said goodbye to our neighbors, walked out of the apartment, and took the subway to Grand Central Station to come west.

I have never forgotten the happy Bronx days.

1980

I Remember

ANDREW J. INGENITO

Andrew J. Ingenito brings alive the sights and sounds of the Morris Park area, where he grew up, highlighted by a recollection of the Morris Park racetrack when it was used for air shows and automobile races.

My age is seventy-eight. I would like to tell what I remember about the area of the old Morris Park racetrack and the adjacent area of Westchester village.

Our family moved from New Jersey, where I was born in 1899, to Lincoln Street, now known as Hone Avenue. My remembering begins when I was about five years old, when I saw a big picture of a Japanese soldier on a horse with a big sword in his hand, in the newspaper. My father told me about the Japanese and Russian war, in which the Japanese were victors.

Our house was right across the New Haven Railroad tracks from Morris Park. My aunt and uncle lived a short distance away, on the same street. I remember one day one of my cousins took me for a walk to show me the firewatch tower at Williamsbridge Road and Pelham Parkway. It was about five stories high. We went up the steps to the top. You could see over all the trees in Eastchester Woods, east and north. In all of my readings about The Bronx, this was never mentioned. This was a short distance from Morris Park racetrack, on the east side.

About 1905, we moved to Dean Place, which was just two blocks from Bear Swamp Road, which is now Bronxdale Avenue at the junction of Sackett Avenue.

The house that we moved into was about two hundred feet from the Morris Park racetrack fence. At that time, I watched when they knocked down the New Haven Railroad bridge over Bear Swamp Road to build a new bridge with steel girders. The bridges had been widened to six railroad tracks. This was done because they were going to electrify the railroad.

I remember seeing one horse race before they closed the racetrack to move to Belmont in Long Island. A number of years before they cut the track into lots, they had auto races and airplanes.

The first airplane to fly at Morris Park was a plane built by Glenn Curtiss. The people watched him for days before he flew. He would push the plane up to the beginning of the home stretch. Then he would come down the home stretch and fly off the ground a few feet. One day, he came down the track and left the ground and flew around the whole racetrack.

Sometimes he would let some men hold the plane while he warmed the engine. That was when we youngsters had a chance to hold the plane. The plane's supports were made of bamboo. The wing covering was made of some kind of cloth which looked like silk.

I do not remember seeing him fly again. He must have flown away one day while I was away, because I was always at the track after school.

After Glenn Curtiss, I saw a single-wing plane come in and land. It was a French plane, and the pilot was in the open and had no cover over him. I think the plane was a Blériot.

The next thing I saw was a small airship driven by a propeller and built like the Goodyear blimp. The blimp had a steel pipe frame. The pilot sat on the frame next to the motor under the center of the blimp. He was also in the open air with no cover. He landed in the center of the track.

I remember seeing the start of a very large airship, which they say went up a little above the ground. I saw all of the steel pipe that was used in a lot on Morris Park Avenue, one block away from the racetrack.

I remember when they tried to fly gliders, which were built like kites. The builder would have one of the local young men lie on the glider to try to fly it. They had a rope attached to a motorcycle, which would pull the glider down the home stretch of the track. The glider would go a short distance, then flop down on the ground. Nobody got killed.

I remember a man who built a machine that he thought would fly without wings. This was a forerunner of the helicopter. This machine was built on a steel frame, with four small wheels. Part of the frame was built on an angle of about thirty degrees. On this part there were about fifty eight-inch-diameter fans interconnected by steel roller chains to a gasoline motor. I saw this run once. It never left the ground.

I remember the twenty-four-hour Vanderbilt cup automobile race. The racetrack had no electric lights, but they had cans with carbide lights which generated acetylene gas for illumination, like the carbide headlights used on automobiles at that time.

I remember a match auto race between a Stanley steamer and a gasoline race car driven by Barney Oldfield. The Stanley steamer ran away from Barney.

I remember an auto race between a Mr. Kelsey in one car and his wife in another car. His wife's auto, on the home stretch turn, went over an embankment and turned over and she and her driver were killed. The Fordham Hospital ambulance, pulled by a horse, came to the accident.

I remember, one Saturday, a large balloon filled with hot air, with a fire built for getting hot air to fill the bag. The hot air went through a covered trough and into the balloon. This balloon did not have a basket; it just had a trapeze for a man to sit on. They let us young boys and some men hold the ropes that were to hold it down until the bag was full of hot air. When the bag was ready to fly, a man came around to tell us when to let the ropes go. He found that my younger brother had tied himself with the rope. My brother nearly went up with the balloon. Then the man sat on the bar of the trapeze with a parachute. The balloon went up toward Pelham Parkway. Then a man shot a pistol off and the balloonist dropped off in the chute. The balloon went over Eastchester Woods and disappeared.

I remember a building was built to construct airplanes. In a lot a short distance back of where we lived, they had a small plane almost finished when one night the building caught fire. It burned to the ground. All the people in the six houses nearby had their garden hoses wetting down the backs of their houses so they would not get on fire. I don't remember a fire hydrant in our area. This building was about two hundred feet from the Morris Park track's wooden fence, where Sackett Avenue now runs through.

I remember a tunnel under Bear Swamp Road. It was used to take the horses off the railroad cars in the Van Nest freightyard. The inclined ramp came up to the racetrack, a short distance from the back of the clubhouse. In the winter, the ramp was good for sledding. Nobody could ever make the turn at the bottom of the ramp. You would always hit the stone wall. You can still see the stone blocks of the entrance to the tunnel on the west side of Bronxdale Avenue. The yard is now occupied by the Con Edison electric company.

I remember the time all the stables in Morris Park burned down. My father always took us to the movies on Sunday. When we came out, we saw the smoke from the fire. There was a very strong wind blowing. My father took us to see the fire. The fireman had to bring the hose over the New Haven tracks. The Boston express was stopped. One fire engine was caught between two stables and was burned. The blowing sparks set fire to the wooden steeple of the Methodist Church on Walker Avenue (now Tremont Avenue). The flying sparks also set fire to the Public School 12 outhouse. P.S. 12 had no toilets in the school building. The school was about a mile from the fire. The next day, after school, we went to look at the burnt stables. They were all burned down, from a short distance from Pelham Parkway right down to near the New Haven Railroad.

I remember a troop of Zouaves with their picturesque uniforms, with red pantaloons, blue jackets, and red Turkish hats, practicing marching in front of the racetrack clubhouse. In looking up the word "Zouave" in the dictionary, I found a note saying a volunteer U.S. regiment, with this type of uniform, fought in the Civil War.

I remember the Interborough Baseball League, consisting of six teams. The Senators came from Unionport, the Franklins and the Cherrys played in Westchester, the Morris Park team came from Van Nest, the Sunsets came from the St. Lawrence Avenue area. The soldiers' team from Fort Schuyler came to play on the Cherry field sometimes. A team from St. Joseph's Deaf and Dumb School also came to play. They had a pitcher named "Dummy" Deegan, who pitched for the Giants at one time.

1977

The Grand Concourse

The construction of the Grand
Concourse often caused
inconvenience to the residents of
the few houses near its path—as it
did to those who lived in six frame
structures north of 165th Street
and south of McClellan Street,
circa 1902. The regrading of the
roadway created a sheer cliff in
front of the houses, making access
difficult, but a temporary solution
was provided by the construction
of wooden stairways.

ABOVE: An eastward view toward the Concourse on May 24, 1907, shows the construction of the transverse road tht would carry Tremont Avenue under the wide boulevard. The great building project has obviously disturbed the tranquil tree-filled community of substantial frame houses.

BELOW: On September 26, 1909, the Concourse was nearing completion. Here, the tunnel that would carry traffic along 175th Street under the new boulevard is under construction.

ABOVE: A 1909 view from 163rd Street and the newly completed Grand Concourse looking southwest reveals a triangular plot of land marking the entrance of the Grand Concourse at 161st Street, which was officially designated the Concourse Plaza. The Lorelei Fountain, honoring German poet Heinrich Heine, was placed on the site in 1899.

BELOW: A stone bridge carrying the newly completed Concourse spanned 175th and 176th streets. Rock outcroppings can be seen on either side of the roadway at the end of the span in this 1910 photograph. The center of the Concourse was a turf track for horses and carriages, while the side roadways were paved. The substantial frame houses of Tremont can be seen in the central distance. The tallest building to the right is the Medical Arts Building.

The Grand Concourse just north of Fordham Road showed signs of change, circa 1925. The street is newly paved in response to the increased preference for automobiles over horses and carriages for transportation. Older electric lamps (seen in the foreground on the traffic islands) are being replaced by newer streetlamps (visible in the distance), which suspended their lighting source on either side of the islands. Recently built five- and six-story apartment houses have eliminated most of the older single-family frame homes, one of which still stands to the right. The open space in the middle right is Poe Park, in which can be seen the Edgar Allan Poe Cottage.

Bronx Memories: 1913–1923

JULIUS G. ROTHENBERG

Julius G. Rothenberg was a member of one of the first Jewish families that moved to The Bronx in the period. Here he recalls his childhood in the rapidly urbanizing Morrisania neighborhood. Then he moved to the quiet, still rural area of Throggs Neck, and his experiences changed dramatically. Nevertheless, the quality of life was remarkably similar in both places.

My first memories of The Bronx go back to when my father opened up a grocery-delicatessen at 1158 Boston Road and we moved into a flat behind it, at 1157 Jackson Avenue. Fire vehicles were horse-drawn in those days, with powerful and thrilling horses in a team of three, and always a Dalmatian dog along, which we knew then only as "fire dogs." Whenever they made their appearance, we would play "fire engine" and would be at once the driver, the engine, and the horses. The Concourse was then known as Grand Boulevard and Concourse, and on a Sunday, the more wealthy would drive their horses and carriages along the dirt road which paralleled the automobile road and which ultimately was added to it.

It always thrilled me somehow to watch the little Italian lamplighter whose approach I always awaited as it began to grow dark. He would come along with a short ladder and a kind of rod with which he would light each streetlamp along the way. I would watch him getting smaller and smaller, my first example of infinity, till I could no longer make him out. He reminded me of the Old Dutch cleanser which Pop had on his shelves, for on the label was a woman who held in her hand a can of Old Dutch Cleanser too. And the can in her hand showed a smaller woman holding a still smaller can of Old Dutch cleanser. The steadily diminishing progression fascinated me.

A vaudeville theater opened up right across the way, and I would sometimes catch a glimpse of the acts through some side exit momentarily opened. There was an exciting Buffalo Bill Wild West Show there for some time, with cowboys and Indians riding their mounts along Boston Road, to my great delight. Once, one of the tradesmen doing business with my father came over to the store on a snowy Sunday, put me on his horse-drawn sleigh, wrapped me in a warm bear rug, and gave me a wonderful ride. Now I see just such vehicles adorning people's suburban lawns. Oh, yes, those were still the immigrant days. We always had room, at least for six months, for a *landsman,* or person from the same part of Europe, if he was a "greener," or greenhorn. We would set out, either in the kitchen or in the entrance hall of the flat, a folding cot for him to sleep on. Then we'd arrange to have him attend the nearest night school, help him find a job, and maybe even a wife. Within six months, he'd be on his feet, earning his living, speaking some English, and maybe courting.

My mother brought over her sister, now my last living European relative, and brought her and my father's half-brother together in marriage lasting almost fifty years and ending in his passing. He would sing Hungarian songs while courting, and I had one of them sung for me by Gypsies a few years ago, when I visited Hungary. We even had Gypsies play for us at one of our weddings. There were no catered affairs then; each woman brought along her special spices, a rolling pin, an apron, and the makings of her favorite dish, and the women vied with each other, while I went from neighbor's oven to neighbor's oven to sample the steaming delicacies.

McKinley Square seemed a long way off in those days, but I found, on returning there as a grown man, that the distance had shrunken considerably. So did the desk at the Morrisania library, where I applied as soon as I could write my name. I even washed my hands thoroughly, clear up to the wrist, mind you, for the librarian checked whether you were worthy of borrowing "li-berry" books.

Pop was no businessman. A great store chain set up a store nearby, and we moved to the corner of Crotona Parkway and Bronx Park South. Pop gave me a job delivering breakfast orders for a nickel a day. Ward's Tip Top bread was a nickel, too, then, and you could buy six small rolls, delivered by me, for a nickel. (Oh, yes; that reminds me: Newspapers went up when we had a store on Boston Road—*Times, American, Journal, World, Tribune,* etc.—from a penny to two cents. Pop was fit to be tied. "Do you realize that this is an increase of one hundred percent!" he would exclaim. I never dared ask him how else they could have increased the price.) I had seen the kids ice skating at the northern end of Bronx Park, on a pond, so I saved up sixty-five cents to buy a pair of clamp ice skates. Unfortunately, a neighbor's boy had a bad fall on roller skates and, if I heard aright, developed "spinal menin-Jesus," so I was forbidden to buy them.

Now we moved to 166th Street, west of Washington Avenue. To the west of us, on Brook Avenue, was a small colony of blacks, who were quiet and minded their own business. One day, a black boy of my age came along where we were playing—normally, they never came our way. The other boys, to my shock, harassed him.

"Are you Jewish?" he asked us. We said we were. "Then you ought to have more understanding." We found it quite ridiculous. "What does being Jewish have to do with it?" It was only as an adult that I came to understand and to appreciate this black boy's precocious wisdom.

(But if, from Bronx Park South, where I formerly lived, I would go with other kids a bit north and west, we would get the same treatment. There were enclaves of one ethnic group here, and another, different ethnically, there, and woe betide whoever drifted where he didn't "belong.")

I remember how we made soap box wagons from discarded baby carriages and wooden cases, far more frequent then. When there were food shows at the nearby armory on Franklin Avenue, we could make a few pennies by delivering the parcels of food bought there. There were also "push-o's," made from a single roller skate separated into halves, one front and one back. They were nailed to the bottom side of a two-by-four. On the top, to the front, was nailed a soap box, and on the top of the soap box two slats, diagonally nailed, as handlebars. They made an awesome noise along the cobbled streets. We would also make a "chicken needs more corn" game from a small wooden cheese box, cutting out square notches, some small, some large, with numbers written above the notches. The smaller the hole, the more marbles we paid to those taking chances. They had to stand at a certain distance from the box and try to roll their marbles through the notched spaces. The owner of the box sat on the sidewalk, his legs spread out to hold the box in between them, and fatten his pockets with the marbles that found no entrance. We also played two different games with marbles.

And we played cat. The small fry played a simplified variation, with a short piece of flat wood, or cat, and a longer piece for hitting the cat. As the cat was in the air, it had to be hit again with the stick, this time for the longest distance possible. Bigger boys used a broom handle of hard wood. A six-inch cut-off, tapered at one end, was used as the cat. While the small fry had to set the cat on a curbstone to loft it, the bigger boys would have to hit the tapered end resting on the pavement to do so. We played between sewers, caught the cat on the fly in order to get "up." We would measure the distance by making the longer stick progress from the starting sewer and walking the stick end over end till we reached the spot where the uncaught cat had landed, counting the number of lengths' distance. Mothers used to scream "holy murder," for the cat had an affinity for babies in carriages. Cops would break up the game if mothers complained. Ten years ago, I discovered that one form of marbles we played was still being played in central Italy, and cat was being played yet in Sicily. Like so many other games I knew as a boy, and that includes girls' games, they are unknown to the present generation of children.

Next, to economize, we moved into an old wooden private house just a block south. It was my job to chop kindling wood for our kitchen range. In the back of this private house was a bit of land, where the tenants had tiny truck gardens. A stablehand who, like Pop, worked for the Schultz Baking Co., around the corner, lived in another private house in the back. He introduced Pop to these wonderful truck gardens, saying, as he made a gesture up to his jawbone, "Bohne bis hie' her!" (Beans 'way up to here!) Evenings, he would go out with his growler for beer, and drink and quarrel with his wife. I think the beer might have been fifteen cents a quart then. During the war years (1917–1918), when coal was scarce, I would go with my wagon to a railroad—where, I no longer recall—in search of lumps of coal along the rails. When we moved to Throggs Neck (1919), then country, I was bitter about the great pile of wood which I had chopped and which Pop saw fit to leave behind.

Throggs Neck proved a fascinating place, though for me it was also lonely. There used to be a gag about the quietest place, between a cemetery and a deaf-and-dumb home, but that describes the location of the house my parents bought, two-family brick, for $3,500 all told, between St. Raymond's Cemetery and St. Joseph Institute for the Deaf. It was on Gifford Avenue near Swinton. I would buy milk, yellow and creamy, and fresh vegetables at Behren's farm, on the site of the present Reade's outdoor theater. I went to P.S. 14 at 3041 Eastern Boulevard. The janitor would ring a church bell to summon us to school, and children came from more distant places, such as Ferry Point and Pennyfield and Fort Schuyler, some in old-style (for them) buses, and some—honestly!—in an old-time Western-type stagecoach hauled by a team of two jackasses. Eastern Boulevard had no sidewalks then, just a dirt lane, which magically was plowed before it was time to go to school, if there was a snowfall. I learned that the "good fairy" who did this public service was the childless Farmer Behrens.

I was then in the eighth year in school. Eight-A and Eight-B were conducted in the same room and by the same teacher, a very able but sartorially careless teacher, Bernard Kelly, whom, somehow, we spoke of as "Nick." He would wear two different-colored socks and often would have one unwedded buttonhole on the bottom of his vest and one unwedded button at the top. He, too, remained unwed. In the spring of 1920, I was in the graduating class, consisting of twelve pupils. Three were left back; one was given a diploma on the promise that he would not attempt to get into high school; and, if you will excuse my bragging, I was made valedictorian, and another boy, salutatorian, of the nine graduates. Told that it was a goodbye speech, I wrote a brief and totally inadequate address and showed it to Mr. Kelly. He sighed and said, "I suppose that now I will again have to write a valedictory speech." The next day, he came in with it, quoting from many American poetry and prose writers, all in his distinctive longhand. "Now take this into Dr. Moore and see whether he approves of it."

I did so, Dr. Moore looked at it, read it approvingly, and asked me, "Did you write this valedictory?"

What could I say? "Yes, sir."

"It's very good. Tell Mr. Kelly it's very good."

There was a fine woods across Eastern Boulevard, and all sorts of wildflowers and berries to gather. The best were the sweet strawberries. A brook flowed pretty parallel to Eastern Boulevard, and one winter we dammed it, burned down the weeds, and prayed for weather cold enough to enable us to ice skate. When our pond froze, people came from everywhere to ice skate. We all had clamp skates, which, at the slightest attempt to do a spread-eagle or some other movement, would come loose and go flying along the icy surface. And sometimes we'd skate on the marginally frozen water of the flatlands near the creek, between Behren's farm and Unionport. South of Balcom Avenue was a city dump where a buddy of mine and I would go scavenging. Tomatoes and asparagus grew there, and squash, and my buddy would take some home. I myself looked for clockworks and other mechanical things. A certain weed, quite milky but with leaves more like dandelion leaves, grew along Balcom Avenue. I would take my wagon and sickle and cut a mess of them for my ducks and geese. They loved them. And I'd catch an odd killifish or two in the brook and feed them to the ducks and geese, too. We had chickens, too, and rabbits and pigeons, and one of my buddies had a billy goat and a goat cart. Mom used to force-feed the geese. We prized the flesh of the geese, especially the livers. Mom kept the equally prized feathers for pillows and featherbeds and used the feathered wings for cleaning the dinner table of crumbs. At first, I had to take the poultry to Unionport to be ritually slaughtered. Later, it became my job, with an ax and chopping block. I hated it when it involved some bird I was fond of, and would pretend that my mother meant a different one, but I never succeeded. Mother knew which bird was destined for the soup pot. She would rub the goose grease on our chest if we had a cold, and put it in the hot milk if we had a cough. That drink was so disgusting, it discouraged us from keeping a cough very long.

Radio was coming in then, but Pop felt that we couldn't afford the expense of the electricity. But Frau Gruler, on what was later Revere Avenue, had a set, with an ear-trumpet-like "loud speaker," and a big auto battery to power it. I used to listen to the Happiness Boys, Billie Jones and Ernie Hare, at my friend's house, on a crystal set. Later, when we visited *landsleit* in East Harlem, I learned that one could buy a galena crystal, a "catswhisker" (two pigtails of stiff wire), and the makings of a variable condenser at Woolworth's. One also bought a headset and some fine copper wire, which was wound around a Quaker Oats box, set up two sliders to run along the coil, and if we were lucky in finding the right spot with the catswhisker, and the right spots for the sliders, lo! voices and music, the marvel of the era! But my studies suffered, and Pop would be furious.

Eastward from in front of St. Joseph's Institute, on a Sunday morning, Italians from all over would come together with their horses and now-empty wagons, and they would race for money.

We would sometimes get together, form a scrub team—who ever heard of Little Leagues and uniforms in those days?—and play against the younger mutes. After a while we stopped going there because there was always a mute umpire who couldn't hear the tick of a foul ball barely grazing the bat. To him, it was a strike, and disputes had to be conducted on paper, with me elected as scribe. There is no more frustrating thing than to have to argue a hot, disputed call with pencil and paper.

Pop was a great climber, and one day we were picking wild cherries on Eastern Boulevard on Behren's fenceline, high up. We had set out a partially filled sack on one of the pickets, as we gathered more in another sack. Along came some young men and women, and noticing the apparently unattended sack, began to sample its contents. Pop got furious, and I came to hear some of his less usual imprecations, as the uninvited guests kept eating away, totally unconcerned about my father's thunderous oaths. Only when they had had their fill did they start walking off, and then we knew why my father's fine maledictions had been in vain. They started talking with their deft and delicate deaf-mute gestures. They hadn't heard a single word.

On the far side of Eastern Boulevard, between St. Joseph's and Fort Schuyler Road (East Tremont Avenue) rode a man we all admired and revered, a conscientious mounted policeman known as "Lock-'em-up" Reilly. He would go tearing along toward Fort Schuyler Road to make a pinch, and catch his man there at the new and wonderful stoplight. To us, he was the Canadian Northwest Mounted, but to judges, he was that much more work, for which they would abuse him, to our shock and disgust.

My bachelor uncle, Morris, would sometimes come to visit. One day, he put on his even-then-old-fashioned bathing suit, with half-sleeves like a T-shirt, and horizontal stripes, and trunks almost down to his knees. He wanted to go bathing. "Put a pair of trousers on over your trunks," Mother warned him, but he wouldn't listen. Later, there was a phone call: He had been penned up at the Fort Schuyler Road police booth and we had to fetch him his trousers and money.

Talking about money, I would earn some with a watering can, a hand cultivator, a trowel, and grass shears, by planting flowers or trimming the graves for people visiting their late loved ones. One Decoration Day, the best day for making money, Pop went to get me for lunch, but despite a broken arm, he grabbed another set of equipment and earned himself a bit too, for Workmen's Compensation didn't pay much, and there was no unemployment insurance, Social Security, or the like. Mom was furious as she waited to serve us, but Pop, always a poor earner but a very responsible family man, came home radiant.

My brother, twelve years younger, was very sick, and a neighbor heard an owl hooting. She knew he would die, from this unmistakable omen. But he's still alive at this writing.

A regular "Toonerville trolley" used to operate between Eastern Boulevard and Westchester Square, on Tremont Avenue, with a highly colorful one-man operator. That trolley would make a beautiful write-up, if someone—not I—could recapture its distinctive atmosphere.

1974

I Grew Up with The Bronx

BERT SACK

Bert Sack remembers his early days in his native Hunt's Point neighborhood, recording in rich detail day-to-day life at the beginning of the twentieth century. His account is especially notable in that he was privileged to witness the construction of the subway and the beginnings of the vast changes it wrought.

The party was over, and the guests were putting on their gaiters and mufflers. My uncle went to get a lantern to light the way to the trolley car. Outside it was still, with only a dog's bark to break the silence of the night. This pastoral picture was not way out in the "sticks," but in The Bronx about the year 1900. It has been my good fortune to live through and witness the vast growth and changes in The Bronx since the early 1900s.

The good old days in The Bronx—what were they like? I was there, I saw, and I remember. Imagine walking ten blocks for an ice cream soda. I did. I had to walk from Fox Street to Zeman's at McKinley Square and to Steiner's bakery next door to it for cake for Sunday's company. We did have a bakery nearby on Home Street, run by Mr. Wilde, where rye bread was sold at four cents for a small and eight cents for a large loaf. I recall a day when my grandmother gave me a quarter to get milk down the street. The owner, by error, gave me twenty-five cents' worth of milk instead of the quart I was supposed to get. My grandmother nearly raised the roof of the store because milk sold at about four cents a quart and she did not know what she would do with five extra quarts.

The family shopping was done on Saturdays. We went down to Third Avenue, which in those days was already the Hub of the Bronx—with a difference. The main stores were located from 142nd Street to 150th Street. There were Weisbart's and Rogers' department stores, Hitchcock's fish market, Rafter's coffee and tea market, the Westchester Clothing Store, and Blackman's sporting goods and stationery store. Fellows and Smith were on the site of the present Hearn's store, and across the street was Lyons and Chabot department store. Fried's was up at about 153rd Street. Furniture row, which included such stores as Guttag's, Piser's, Fennel's, and Bauman's, was at 150th Street and Westchester Avenue.

Recreation was as simple in those days as transportation was difficult. A favorite pastime on a summer Sunday afternoon was to visit the neighbors' gardens. Besides the gardens, nearly all our neighbors had some kind of fruit trees, and when they ripened, we would swap fruit. Our backyard had two cherry trees, planted by my uncles. Our nearest neighbors, the Clemenses, had a pear tree. Others had peach trees and grape arbors. The only theater I remember in those days was the Metropolis, at 142nd Street and Third Avenue, which ran a stock company. Oh, yes, there was a penny arcade at about 148th Street and Third Avenue. The nearest vaudeville house was the Alhambra, at 126th Street in Manhattan.

Transportation, while rugged, was cheap. The fare was, of course, five cents, and for three cents more, we received a transfer to the Third Avenue El. The original terminus of the El was at 129th Street, which was also the end of the line for most trolley routes in the Bronx. The original trolley lines, as I remember them, were the Boulevard (or Huckleberry) line; Westchester Avenue line; Boston Road line; Webster Avenue line; 161st Street line; Sedgwick Avenue line, which started at 161st Street and Third Avenue; and Tremont Avenue line. West Farms Square was the terminus of lines coming down from the north: the Mount Vernon, West Mount Vernon, White Plains Avenue, and Williams Bridge lines. Long before the auto, Bronxites took Sunday trips into the country by trolley car to such places as Glen Island, Rye Beach, and Hudson Park. Some of these trips took hours and required many fares. A popular recreation spot for Bronxites was North Beach. In order to get there, we boarded a boat at Port Morris at about 136th Street and the East River.

A favorite sport today is skiing, but it cannot compare with riding down the hill on a toboggan on Fox Street at breakneck speed three blocks almost up to Freeman Street. The snow and ice brought fun, but also woe to us in those days. A heavy snowstorm would not only slow up the trolley cars, but often would knock down the overhead wires, and no cars could run. The only way then to get home was to use "shanks' mare" (our own two feet). Many a time during the winter our gas line would freeze up and my uncles would have to thaw it out. With all this, the clean, white snow and Jack Frost's handiwork made the winter beautiful.

Another way for a family to enjoy the outdoors was to hire a surrey and drive up to Thwaites in City Island for shore dinner. Dinner must have been a lot cheaper then, because we could afford to bring about eight of us in the carriage to Thwaites.

One of our neighbors, Mr. John De Hart, an architect who planned many of the local houses, including the one I was born in, had a pony cart with wicker-back seats, and often took me for a ride. One Sunday, after he had just bought a steam car, he took me for my first auto ride. That was a real thrill. Mr. Gaffney, who later built about fifty small houses in our part of The Bronx, also got a steamer, and his and Mr. De Hart's were the only autos in the neighborhood for a long time.

While the lower Bronx around 138th Street was well built up, our section was still rural. Prospect Avenue seemed to be the dividing line, though even there, there were many fine houses set back with large lawns. Coming down the hill from Prospect Avenue on the Westchester Avenue trolley, we would see farms stretching southward almost to 156th Street, and northward to Tiffany Street. Tiffany, Vyse, Fox, Hoe, Bristow, and Chisholm were all names taken from the many estates which were to the south and north of Westchester Avenue. Where the Loew's Boulevard theater now stands, I picked many sweet Seckel pears. There were natural springs at the Hunt's Point Avenue station of the New Haven Railroad. Later, a business-minded fellow put in a pipe and sold the water to the nearby families who sent their servant girls there with bottles each evening.

Another mode of travel in my early days was the stagecoach. A day's picnic was spent at Hunt's Point by taking a coach at what is now Crames Square. We had our choice of going to either Barretto or Hunt's Point. Another coach went to Clason Point, starting about one block south of where the St. Lawrence subway station is now. A large stagecoach holding about forty left Westchester Square for Pelham Bay Park or for Lohbauer's for clambakes.

Commercially, in those days, The Bronx was the piano hub of the country. Centering around 138th Street were the factories of Pease, Waters, Newby, and Evans, and many others. The brewing industry was well represented by many plants on St. Ann's Avenue, including Eblings and Hupfels; and up on Third Avenue between 168th and 169th Streets were Mayers, Eichlers, and others. Eblings used to age their beer in caves under Eagle Avenue. When we thought of beer in those days, we also thought of beer gardens and picnic grounds. There were many, including Hoffman's, Zeltner's at 170th Street and Third Avenue, one at 149th Street and St. Ann's Avenue, and another at Prospect Avenue and 167th Street.

When two of my aunts and an uncle first came to Fox Street, they had to walk across fields to get to P.S. 90 at 163rd Street and Eagle Avenue because no streets had been laid out between Fox Street and the school. The principal then was Evander Childs, whose name is immortalized by the Evander Childs High School. My schooling started at P.S. 20 at 167th Street. The school was built at the request of the property owners of the neighborhood, who went down to the Board of Education in 1895 to ask for it. It was built in 1896, the year I was born. In my day, when there was a storm or bad weather, Miss Mary A. Curtis, the principal of P.S. 20, kept us in school till two-thirty, instead of sending us home for lunch at twelve o'clock. I was lucky because my grandmother would come across the street from our house with a sandwich for me. The original building of P.S. 20 was only two stories high, but later, the first annex was added. I had the unique pleasure of speaking last year in the original assembly room of the school I had attended nearly sixty years before. When The Bronx started to grow, a new school was built on Longwood Avenue; Mrs. Lichtenstein was the principal. The population was so small, the school opened practically without pupils.

All this rural atmosphere could not last forever. In 1903, I watched the building of the elevated structure of the subway on Southern Boulevard from our window on Fox Street. The next year, 1904, the subway started operating, but not in The Bronx. The terminus was at 145th Street and Lenox Avenue. In the meantime, the Second Avenue El came up by a spur at 149th Street as far as Freeman Street. Finally, about 1905, through service was opened to Bronx Park by subway.

This was the beginning of the end of The Bronx as the home of farms and estates. The Tiffanys, Foxes, and all the other old families soon abandoned their homes. Many streets, such as Fox, Tiffany, and Kelly, which had ended at Westchester Avenue, were cut through to Intervale Avenue. A Sunday pastime then was the inspection of the new flats being built. One of the first was at the northwest corner of Simpson Street and Westchester Avenue. The first real estate boom was started by the American Real Estate Company, who built at Westchester Avenue from Simpson Street to Southern Boulevard. They also built a large house at 163rd Street between Fox and Simpson streets. This was, for a long time, the only house on 163rd Street from Intervale Avenue to Southern Boulevard. It did not take long before the rest of Simpson, Fox, Tiffany, and Kelly streets were filled with flats. The change had started. Southern Boulevard, which had boasted of one building between Westchester Avenue and 163rd Street, an annex for P.S. 20, soon became a marketplace.

The building boom also brought about an ethnic change. The first newcomers were German-American families. Soon, they were displaced by many Jewish families from Harlem. Following them came the Jewish people from the East Side. During World War II, another change started. The colored people and Spanish-speaking folks came, and now the neighborhood is well mixed with all races and nationalities.

1964

The Growing Metropolis

The southwest corner of 192nd Street and Kingsbridge Road, circa 1904, shows signs of the recent regrading of the street. The frame houses in the center of the photograph are on Valentine Avenue; the last one on the row is still under construction. On the horizon at the right can be seen the faint image of a building with a cupola, which is the Catholic Orphan Asylum on Kingsbridge Road near Sedgwick Avenue.

ABOVE: After the demise of the Jerome Park racetrack, most of its site was used for the Jerome Park reservoir, whose excavation is seen in 1905 from the pumping station. Most of the laborers constructing the reservoir were Italian immigrants. The Van Cortlandt Park parade ground is in the open area in the center background. Van Cortlandt Lake is to the right of the parade ground, below Vault Hill. The Palisades of New Jersey are on the horizon.

BELOW: On East 149th Street, in 1905, local residents came out to observe the final work as a new concrete foundation was being laid in the street.

The Hunt's Point peninsula, near the eastern end of 149th Street, was an area busy with construction in 1905. The steel frame of a large electric generating plant is rising near the water's edge. The roadway, atop which three men are standing, is being extended and elevated over the railway tracks. The tall, tapering column rising between the sets of tracks is a sewer ready for the extension of the street. North Brother Island with its complex of hospitals lies offshore to the left.

In 1908, at Westchester Avenue,
looking north from Freeman Street
at Edgewater Road, a trolley can
be seen crossing the bridge over
the Bronx River. The mounted
policeman is observing workmen
who are improving the street.

ABOVE: The Bureau of Highways and Sewers building at 180th Street and Webster Avenue, whose courtyard is seen in this 1910 photograph, was where water wagons were constructed. The wagons were used to wash manure off the streets and to keep the dust down on dirt roads.

BELOW: The interior of the Bureau of Highways and Sewers building in 1910 shows the water tanks which were used to wash the streets and which were repaired in this shop lined along the wall to the left.

A nearly completed step street,
seen here circa 1910, would enable
pedestrians to climb the steep,
rocky slope from Webster Avenue
at 187th Street to Marion Avenue.
The newer apartment houses at the
above right contrast with the older
single-family frame homes to the
left.

In the Bronx Borough Hall, in
Crotona Park at Tremont and
Third avenues, the office of the
borough president was on the
second floor in the wing to the
right of the main entrance. The
bunting is affixed to the building to
celebrate the twin occasions of Flag
Day and Bronx Borough Day on
June 14, circa 1925.

Index

Index

Index

Index

About the Editors

LLOYD ULTAN is a professor of history at the Edward Williams College of Fairleigh Dickinson University in Hackensack, New Jersey. He served as president of The Bronx County Historical Society from 1971 to 1976, and is the author of several articles and books on Bronx history, including the highly acclaimed *The Beautiful Bronx (1920–1950)*.

GARY HERMALYN is the executive director of The Bronx County Historical Society and president of The History of New York City Project. A well-known lecturer and author on New York City history, he received his doctorate from Columbia University.

The Bronx County Historical Society

The Bronx County Historical Society was founded in 1955 for the purpose of promoting knowledge, interest, and research in The Bronx. The Society administers The Museum of Bronx History, Edgar Allan Poe Cottage, a research library, and The Bronx County Archives; publishes a varied series of books, journals, and newsletters; conducts historical tours, lectures, courses, school programs, and commemorations; designs exhibitions; sponsors various expeditions; and produces the "Out of the Past" radio show and cable T.V. programs. The society is active in furthering the arts and in preserving the natural resources of The Bronx and in creating the sense of pride in the Bronx community.